At Fort Stevens Salmon Charters, Hammond, Oregon

National Geographic's Driving Guides to America

Pacific Northwest
Oregon, Washington, and Alaska

By Bob Devine
Photographed by Phil Schofield

Prepared by
The Book Division
National Geographic Society
Washington, D.C.

**National Geographic's
Driving Guides To America
Pacific Northwest**

By BOB DEVINE
Photographed by PHIL SCHOFIELD

Published by
THE NATIONAL GEOGRAPHIC SOCIETY

Reg Murphy
President and Chief Executive Officer
Gilbert M. Grosvenor
Chairman of the Board
Nina D. Hoffman
Senior Vice President

Prepared by The Book Division

William R. Gray
Vice President and Director
Charles Kogod
Assistant Director
Barbara A. Payne
Editorial Director

Driving Guides to America

Elizabeth L. Newhouse
*Director of Travel Books
and Series Editor*
Cinda Rose
Art Director
Thomas B. Powell III
Illustrations Editor
Caroline Hickey, Barbara A. Noe
Senior Researchers
Carl Mehler
Map Editor and Designer

Staff for this book

Sean M. Groom
Project Manager
Mary Luders
Text Editor
Thomas B. Powell III
Illustrations Editor
Cinda Rose
Art Director
Carl Mehler
Map Editor and Designer

Karin L. Hayes
Caroline Hickey
Michael H. Higgins
Keith R. Moore
Researchers

Barbara A. Noe
Contributing Editor

Paulette L. Claus
Editorial Consultant

Thomas L. Gray, Joseph F. Ochlak,
Tracey M. Wood
Map Researchers
Michelle H. Picard, Martin S. Walz,
Tracey M. Wood, and Mapping
Specialists, Inc.
Map Production
Tibor G. Tóth
Map Relief

Meredith C. Wilcox
Illustrations Assistant
Richard S. Wain
Production Project Manager
Lewis R. Bassford, Lyle Rosbotham
Production

Kevin G. Craig, Mark Fitzgerald,
Dale M. Herring, Peggy J. Purdy
Staff Assistants

Susan Fels
Indexer

Mary Jennings
Contributor

**Manufacturing
and Quality Management**

George V. White, *Director*
John T. Dunn, *Associate Director*
Vincent P. Ryan, *Manager*

Cover: Cannon Beach from Ecola State Park, Oregon

Previous pages: Wonder Lake in Denali National Park, Alaska
STEFAN SCHOTT/KEN GRAHAM AGENCY

Facing page: Backpacker along Copper Ridge Trail, Mount Redoubt in background, North Cascades N.P., Washington

4

Contents

6

Alaska

0   100 mi
0   150 km

Bays to Baker
Bellingham
BRITISH COLUMBIA   CANADA
U.S.
NORTH CASCADES N.P.
North Cascades ★
Washington's Waterfront
★★
20   97   395
5
2
101
Everett   **Heart of the
Cascades** ★
Spokane
OLYMPIC   101
N.P.   2
2
Seattle   90
WASHINGTON   Spokane
Loop
★★ **Olympic
Peninsula**   Tacoma
Olympia   ★
90   395   195
MOUNT
RAINIER N.P.
**Southwest
Corner**   6   12   **Around** ★
Mt. Rainier   **Walla Walla
Wander**   12
Astoria   4   82
30   Longview   97   Richland   **Walla Walla**
★★   Portland   5   14   **Grand
Gorge**   12
**Northwest
Corner**   6
★ **Willamette
Valley**   The
Dalles   206   Pendleton
97   **North
Central
Backroads**   84   82
★ **Mt.
Hood
Loop** 26   218   **The
Wallowas**
101
Salem   Baker   86
City
**Central
Coast**   20   **Central
Oregon**   84
★ **and
South
Valley**   5   Eugene   Bend   395   26
126
20   Burns   20
Coos
Bay   O R E G O N
★   CRATER LAKE
NATIONAL PARK   78
**South
Coast**   97   **Hidden
Southeast** ★   95
101
5   62   **King Lear to
Crater Lake**   395   205   95
Brookings   Ashland   140   Klamath Falls
CALIFORNIA   NEVADA
IDAHO

Hall of Mosses, Hoh Rain Forest, Washington

8

Does It Ever Stop Raining?

Yes. Contrary to popular opinion, people in Oregon and Washington do sometimes walk down the street without an umbrella. How often depends on where you are. Keep one handy when on the ocean side of the Olympic Peninsula— parts of the coastal plain average about 130 inches a year, making it the wettest place in the contiguous 48. On the other hand, the reputedly deluged cities of Seattle and Portland get only 35 or 40 inches a year, comparable to New York or Chicago. And much of the land east of the Cascades is a desert, receiving less than 10 inches annually. Very little rain falls anywhere in Oregon and Washington in summer and early fall.

/first set eyes on the Pacific Northwest in 1975. My wife and I drove along the Oregon coast on our honeymoon— what could be more romantic than a wild rocky shore framed by forested mountains? This image of the Northwest, held by many Americans, is not inaccurate, but it is incomplete. Just as my relationship with my wife has deepened over the years, so has my connection with the Northwest matured since we came to live here. I got to know many other Northwest landscapes: the bucolic Willamette Valley; the Olympic Peninsula's temperate rain forests; the dramatic gorge carved by the broad Columbia River; Mount Rainier, the volcano that reigns over western Washington; the beautiful backwaters of the San Juan Islands; and the unexpected high desert country of eastern Oregon.

I also discovered the region's sophisticated delights. A world of knowledge embraced me at Powell's City of Books in Portland. A mosaic of Pacific Rim cultures greeted me in Seattle. Tacoma's Washington State History Museum revealed unsuspected nooks of the region's past. Smaller cities and towns offered other charms: little harbors where boats bring pots swarming with crabs; mom-and-pop cafés whose customers wear cowboy hats; and dozens of proud museums that celebrate the Northwest's pioneer history.

Finally, I discovered Alaska. The Great Land, looming on the northwest edge of the Northwest, added a whole new set of cultural, geographical, and historical colors to the region's palette. I saw huge expanses of tundra, dog sleds, grizzly bears, glaciers the size of counties, and vast wildernesses where wolves howl in the moonlight.

So much to see. After living here for many years I now know enough about the Pacific Northwest to realize I'll never know it all. Such an exciting thought.

BOB DEVINE

About the Guides

*N*ATIONAL GEOGRAPHIC'S DRIVING GUIDES TO AMERICA invite you on memorable road trips through the United States and Canada. Intended both as travel planners and companions, each volume guides you on preplanned tours over a wide variety of terrain to the best places to see and things to do. The authors, expert regional travel writers, star-rate (from none to two ★★) the drives and points of interest to make sure you don't miss their favorites.

All distances and drive times are approximate (if you linger, as you should, plan on considerably more time). Recommended seasons are the best times to go, but roads and sites are open all year unless otherwise noted. Besides the stated days of operation, many sites close on national holidays.

For the most up-to-date site information, it's best to call ahead when possible.

Then, with this book and a road map, set off on your adventure through this awesomely beautiful land.

Liberty Falls, Edgerton Highway, Alaska

MAP KEY and ABBREVIATIONS

National Antelope Refuge		
National Estuarine Research Reserve	N.E.R.R	
National Historical Reserve		
National Monument	N.M.	
National Park	NAT. PARK., N.P.	
National Scenic Area	N.S.A.	
National Recreation Area	N.R.A.	
National Volcanic Monument	N.V.M.	
National Forest	NAT. FOR., N.F.	
National Grasslands	N.G.	
State Forest		
Wilderness Area		
National Wildlife Refuge	N.W.R.	
Outstanding Natural Area		
Recreation Land		
State Natural Area	S.N.A	
State Park	S.P.	
State Scenic Corridor		
Indian Reservation	I.R.	

Featured Drive

Interstate Highway
(5)

U.S. Federal Highway
(101)

State Road
(9)

Trans-Canada Highway
(1)

Principal Canadian Highway
(3)

County, Local, or Other Road
(90)

Ferry
FEATURED · · · · OTHER

State or National Border

Boundaries

NAT. FOR.   N.W.R.

Desert Area   Dry Lake   Glacier

■ Point of Interest
★ State or Provincial Capital
| Dam   ) (Pass
+ Elevation, Peak   = Falls

ADDITIONAL ABBREVIATIONS

Cr.	*Creek*
Fk.	*Fork*
I.-s.	*Island-s*
L.	*Lake*
Mt.-s.	*Mount-ain-s*
NAT. MEM.	*National Memorial*
N.H.S.	*National Historical Site*
PT.	*Point*
R.	*River*
S.H.P.	*State Historical Park*
S.H.S.	*State Historic Site*
S.R.A.	*State Recreation Area*
S.R.S.	*State Recreation Site*
S.S.C.	*State Scenic Corridor*
S.S.V.	*State Scenic Viewpoint*
St.-e.	*Saint-e*
Str.	*Strait*

POPULATION

● **Seattle**	500,000 and over
● **Portland**	50,000 to under 500,000
● Oysterville	under 50,000

Hidden Southeast ★

● 330 miles ● 3 days ● Spring through autumn
● No services for the 107 miles between Fields and
Crane. Snow closes Steens Mountain National Back
Country Byway from about November to mid-June.

10

Southeast Oregon seems to belong to another state. The remote, high-desert countryside bears little family resemblance to the coast, the Cascade Range, the Willamette Valley, or any of the state's other better known destinations. This loop takes in the heart of this corner of Oregon, exploring a county that scatters 7,500 residents over an area larger than Vermont. Starting in Burns, the drive plunges south into a landscape of sagebrush flats, ranches, wild horses, and one-street towns. But travelers find surprises, too, such as vast marshes brimming with wildlife, a towering mountain, and a moonscape of cinder cones and lava flows.

In ❶ **Burns** *(Harney County Chamber of Commerce 541-573-2636)* stop at **The Harney County Historical Museum** *(18 W. D St. 541-573-5618. April-Sept. Tues.-Sat.; adm. fee)*. The displays of buffalo rifles, branding irons, and arrowheads seem to impart a deeper meaning here than in a big-city institution, exhibited in a region where many of these artifacts were once put to use. The museum also has its share of the idiosyncratic, including a full-size copy of the Liberty Bell made out of conifer cones, and an exhibit on carbon tetrachloride.

Drive 2 miles east of Burns on Oreg. 78 and then head south on Oreg. 205, passing sagebrush flats and ranches. As you cross over the Narrows (the meeting of Malheur Lake and Mud Lake), keep an eye out for tight formations of white pelicans skimming the water in graceful unison, like synchronized swimmers. About 25 miles from Burns lies the **Malheur National Wildlife Refuge** ★ ★ *(541-493-2612. Refuge and museum daily, Visitor Center Mon.-Fri. and some weekends in spring and summer)*. Take Sodhouse Lane to the refuge headquarters and browse the small but excellent museum, where hundreds of mounted birds, bird eggs, bird nests, and bird wings quickly convey Malheur's status as one of the nation's birding hot spots. Bird-watchers can start their quest by using the spotting scopes at the nearby Visitor Center to survey the lake.

Pick up a refuge map and head south on Oreg. 205. Depending on the season, you may see golden eagles, yellow-headed blackbirds, trumpeter swans, kingfishers, sandhill cranes, herons, pheasants, cinnamon teals, mallards, gadwalls, northern shovelers, and more; some 300 species have been sighted here. Linger and watch as ibises probe the mud with their scimitar bills, or sight some of this verdant area's many mammals.

After about 20 miles, turn east on Diamond Lane for a short trip to **Diamond Craters Outstanding Natural Area** *(Self-guided tour map available at Bureau of Land Management, US 20/395 W of Hines. 541-573-4400).* Passable dirt roads lead motorists to a variety of volcanic features, including domes, lava tubes, spatter cones, and craters. For a close-up view, take a walk around the **Lava Pit Crater,** where the basalt underfoot has assumed the shapes of vertebrae, pancakes, blisters, and other weird forms. Watch for lizards and rattlesnakes around the rim and look for owls and canyon wrens down in the crater itself. For a look at a really small town, continue southeast a few miles to ❷ **Diamond,** with a population of about seven. The

Kiger Mustangs

Wild horses roam several parts of Malheur and the Steens, but travelers should look very closely if they spot horses near Diamond. Do they have zebra stripes on their knees and hocks? Bicolored manes and tails? Face masks or cobwebbing on their faces? These and other traits are characteristic of Kiger mustangs, the nearly pure descendants of the Spanish horses introduced to North America in the 1600s. A herd of 50 to 80 inhabits a 37,000-acre protected area just east of Diamond.

11

Wild horses, Bureau of Land Management processing center, Burns

town mainly consists of the immaculately refurbished 1898 **Hotel Diamond** *(541-493-1898)*, which offers a cozy lobby and wraparound screened-in porch. (Bring bug repellent to Malheur during spring and summer.)

Oreg. 205 south leads to ❸ **Frenchglen,** slightly larger than Diamond, with maybe eight people. It also has its own historic hostelry, the **Frenchglen Hotel** *(541-493-2825. Mid-March–mid-Nov. Reservations advised for dining)*, built in 1916. Whether a guest or not, you can partake of the congenial, family-style dinner.

Frenchglen is the starting point of the **Steens Mountain National Back Country Byway**★★**,** a 55-mile gravel-and-dirt road that loops up and down the west slope of the Steens. (Don't bring a RV or low-clearance vehicle; the route is decent except for a few miles of rough road on the south part of the loop that must be taken at about 10 miles per hour.) The Steens is a 30-mile-long, fault-block mountain, shaped like an ax blade lying on its side. The west side slopes gently, but the east side plunges a mile from the approximately 9,700-foot rim almost straight down to the desert below.

The views from the rim are spectacular, but don't neglect the scenery all around while getting there. The road begins in sagebrush-grassland, rising through the juniper and mountain mahogany zones to aspen territory. Several lovely meadows and lakes lined by quaking aspen invite a stroll. Some of the old aspens bear the images of ships, wine glasses, and coffee pots, carved many decades ago by Basque sheep-herders. The road keeps rising through life zones all the way to subalpine grasslands. Abundant wildflowers throng different zones at different times of year, blooming later and later as you get higher and higher. **Kiger Gorge**★**,** **Little Blitzen Gorge**★**,** and **Big Indian Gorge**★ provide views that rival those from the rim.

Rodeo cowboy, Frenchglen

Don't get so absorbed in the scenery that you forget to watch for wildlife. Pronghorn bound across the lower hillsides while bighorn sheep negotiate the upper reaches. Higher still, eagles, falcons, and other raptors often ride the thermals that rise along the eastern cliffs. Look down to spot

12

the marmots and pikas squeaking and skittering amid the rock piles. Herds of wild horses roam the southern part of the loop, as well as elk, deer, coyotes, and other critters.

From the southern entrance of the Steens Mountain

Viewpoint, Steens Mountain

Byway, the drive continues south on Oreg. 205, passing in the shadows of gnarled cliffs, snaking through arid hills, and skirting the big empty of the **Catlow Valley.** After about 50 miles travelers hit the tiny ranching town of ❹ **Fields,** where life revolves around Fields Station, a combination café/store/gas station. Sometimes small planes from outlying ranches land on the road and taxi up to the gas station for a fill-up. Try one of the café's "world famous" milkshakes—really quite tasty. After buying the shake you can watch as the owners add to the bar graph on the wall; each year they stage a sales competition between shakes and cheeseburgers.

Then head north on Fields-Denio Road toward the Alvord Desert. About 10 miles of dusty driving (the road turns to gravel 2 miles out) brings you to ❺ **Andrews,** where the population numbers one—Cactus Johnny Smyth. Grandson of one of the town's first settlers, this old buckaroo is thought to be its last year-round resident.

Just beyond Andrews, travelers crest a hill and behold the **Alvord Desert★.** From this perspective it's a classic mirage, looking exactly like a lake. But when you pull alongside the desert a few miles later, you can see that it's a white alkali flat. Wade through the sagebrush for a few hundred yards and walk out onto the hard-baked surface of the desert. Get far enough out onto this otherworldly landscape and you'll become pleasantly disoriented. The adventurous can take a short, rutted spur road and drive out onto the Alvord. (Don't try this if it's wet or about to rain. The surface can become so slippery that vehicles get stranded. By the same token, don't drive to the northern part of the Alvord, which is usually soggy.) Motorists can drive 7 miles across the desert to some sand dunes and hills. Because the Alvord is utterly flat and devoid of obstacles, sound judgment sometimes succumbs to temptation and drivers engage in unorthodox behaviors, such as sitting in the back seat while the car cruises on its own, or letting eight-year-olds steer.

Back in the front seat and with an adult at the wheel, continue north to become caught between a rock and a hot place, with the precipitous east side of the Steens looming to the west and the Alvord Desert stretching to the east. Scan the steep slopes for bighorn sheep; several bands inhabit the area. Sometimes afternoon thunderstorms muscle across the Steens, filling the desert below with the smell of wet earth, the bright wink of lightning, and the resonant booms of thunder echoing off the mountain's brawny flanks.

Alkali flat, Alvord Desert

Sixty-five miles out of Fields, the road encounters pavement, Oreg. 78. Follow this northwest for some 40 miles as the highway curves through swelling hills and edges along Malheur's eastern boundary before coming to the little town of ⑥ **Crane.** Its claim to fame is most evident on Friday afternoons, when pickups, cars, and the occasional small plane pull up to the high school and start hauling kids home for the weekend. The rest of the week students stay at school, their far-flung ranch and farm homes too remote to make daily travel practical. This is one of the oldest public boarding high schools in the state. From Crane, a 30-mile run on Oreg. 78 brings you back to Burns.

King Lear to Crater Lake ★★

● **250 miles** ● **3 days** ● **Summer and autumn** ● **Rim Drive at Crater Lake closes mid-October to early July.**

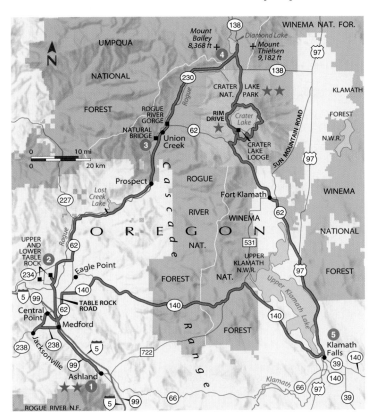

An ambitious traveler could hike the high-country forests of Crater Lake National Park in the morning, admire the outstanding collections of the Favell Museum of Western Art and Indian Artifacts in Klamath Falls in the afternoon, and thrill to the lyrical language of the Oregon Shakespeare Festival in Ashland that evening—although a slower pace is recommended. Instead, begin this varied route amid the theaters, galleries, and museums of Ashland, then follow the Rogue River high into the Cascade Range, pass through Crater Lake National Park, drop down to the wildlife-rich lakes and marshes of the upper Klamath Basin, and cross back over the mountains.

In 1935 a local college professor and his students presented three shows of two Shakespeare plays as part of the Fourth of July celebration in ❶ **Ashland** ★★ *(Chamber of Commerce 541-482-3486).* That launched the **Oregon**

Shakespeare Festival★★ *(541-482-4331. Fee for plays and tours),* for which this pleasant little town is now renowned. Today the festival runs from about mid-February through October. Some 100,000 people come each year to attend more than 700 performances of 11 plays—four by Shakespeare and seven by other playwrights—and enjoy some of the finest regional theater in the nation.

For a pre-play warm-up, loll on the central courtyard lawn and enjoy the free **Green Show**★ *(Mid-June–mid-Oct. on evenings of Elizabethan Theatre performances),* which may include Renaissance dancers in period costumes or musicians playing period instruments. Theater lovers should not miss the backstage tour *(fee),* led by actors and theater workers who provide an insider's view. You'll learn many things during the two-hour ramble, from how a stage manager juggles hundreds of cues to why costume designers use yak hair to make fake beards. Next visit the **Exhibit Center** *(Adm. fee),* which displays props, parts of sets, and other paraphernalia. You can even try on costumes.

The Shakespeare Festival has long been the big frog in the little pond of Ashland, but other attractions do exist. For those who haven't gotten their fill of the performing arts, the **Oregon Cabaret Theatre** *(1st and Hargadine Sts. 541-488-8349. Call for schedule; adm. fee)* offers musicals, revues, and comedies in a converted Baptist Church. Much of the town's attraction stems from its downtown charm, with historic buildings, sidewalk cafés, nearly two dozen art galleries and shops, and a plaza where numerous drinking fountains offer the mineral waters of Lithia Springs.

Lithia Park, Ashland

Art buffs will want to stop by the Southern Oregon University campus and its **Schneider Museum** *(1250 Siskiyou Blvd. 541-552-6245. Tues.-Sat.; donation),* which features changing exhibits of contemporary art from around the U.S.

The town's gathering place, **Lithia Park,** stretches for a mile south from downtown along Ashland Creek. The interpretive Woodland Trail meanders through the park and winds along the bench-lined Lower Duck Pond. Pause here to feed bread

16

Historic main street, Jacksonville

Bozo the Clown

Vance DeBar Colvig—later dubbed "Pinto" because of his freckles—was born in 1892 in Jacksonville; his grandparents came to southern Oregon as pioneers. He worked as a circus clown, a cartoonist, a film-animation artist, and an actor in silent films. But Colvig found his niche when sound came to Hollywood. His versatile voice kept him busy, especially with Disney Studios, which hired him to do voices for Goofy, two of the seven dwarfs, one of the three little pigs, and many others. Colvig even did the barking and growling for Pluto. Then Colvig originated the character of Bozo the Clown, first on records in the 1940s, later playing him on television. Visitors to the Jacksonville Museum of Southern Oregon History can learn all about Colvig next door at the **Children's Museum** (206 N. 5th St. 541-773-6536 ext. 304. Closed Mon.-Tues. Labor Day–Mem. Day; adm. fee).

crumbs to the resident swans or admire the glossy, colorful plumage of the wood ducks. More rugged souls can choose from a host of hikes in the nearby **Rogue River National Forest** *(for maps and information contact Ashland Ranger District 541-482-3333)*, including a jaunt on the Mexico-to-Canada Pacific Crest National Scenic Trail, which passes just outside of town. Nestled at the base of Mount Ashland and surrounded by federally owned land, the town is a jumping-off point for those seeking outdoor adventure. Winter snows attract both downhill and cross-country skiers, and, during warmer months, the Rogue and Klamath Rivers beckon rafters and anglers (contact the Chamber of Commerce for information on outfitters and guides).

To get a good idea of Oregon's pioneer days, drive 15 miles northwest to the small town of **Jacksonville** *(Chamber of Commerce 541-899-8118)*. About 90 buildings date from the 19th century, including the 1873 **Beekman House** *(470 E. California St. Mem. Day–Labor Day; adm. fee),* where docents in period costumes give tours. Artifacts and information about the area's past await in the 1883 county courthouse building, which now holds the **Jacksonville Museum of Southern Oregon History** *(5th and C Sts. 541-773-6536 ext. 301. Closed Mon.-Tues. Labor Day–Mem. Day; adm. fee).* In a more contemporary vein, on various summer evenings the town pulses to the music of the **Britt Festivals**★ *(541-779-0847 or 800-882-7488. Mid-June–early Sept.; adm. fee).* People bearing picnics and blankets settle beneath the pines on Peter Britt's historic estate to listen to performers from B.B. King to Jean-Pierre Rampal.

Travelers who want to go back in time further than

historic Jacksonville—say, a few million years further—can drive to neighboring **Central Point** and tour **Crater Rock Museum**★ *(2002 Scenic Ave. 541-664-6081. Tues., Thurs., and Sat.)*. Like a diamond in the rough, the museum's exterior looks as prepossessing as a warehouse, but its interior sparkles with lavish displays of rocks, gems, fossils, arrowheads, petrified wood, and even dinosaur eggs from China. The friendly docents—members of the Roxy Ann Gem & Mineral Society, who founded and supply the museum—love to show off their remarkable collection.

Continue north of Medford on Table Rock Road. The Table Rocks themselves, about 10 miles up the road, are two basalt-capped buttes rising from the grasslands; they comprise ➋ **Upper** and **Lower Table Rock** *(Bureau of Land Management 541-770-2200)*. Trails wind to the tops of both buttes, where hikers can relish wildflowers, the sweet songs of meadowlarks, vernal pools, and sprawling views.

18

Crater Lake National Park

A few miles north of Oreg. 234, Oreg. 62 joins the **Rogue River** and follows it up into the **Cascades.** Beyond **Lost Creek Lake,** created by the last dam on the Rogue, the river becomes a wild thing that deserves a closer look. A few easy access points exist between Prospect and Union Creek in the **Rogue River National Forest** *(Prospect Ranger District 541-560-3400)*. At ❸ **Natural Bridge,** a mile or so south of Union Creek, the river disappears underground into an ancient lava tube for about 200 feet. A wheelchair-accessible U.S. Forest Service interpretive trail begins here and explains the site. Just north of Union Creek, at the Rogue Gorge Interpretive Site, walk or roll along the paved trail and watch the river thrash through a 40-foot-deep, 25-foot-wide chasm. Hikers can branch off south onto the **Rogue Gorge Trail** ★ and then deep into the old-growth forest on the easy, 4.4-mile **Union Creek Trail.**

Next take Oreg. 230 north to ❹ **Diamond Lake.** Framed by **Mount Bailey** and **Mount Thielsen,** this long, lovely lake is popular among boaters, fishermen, and those who like to sit and stare at lovely lakes. Ambitious hikers can labor to the top of Mount Bailey (8,368 feet), and really ambitious hikers can struggle to Mount Thielsen's spiked summit (9,182 feet), known as the lightning rod of the Cascades (needless to say, don't go during a thunderstorm). The views are astonishing but

Why So Blue?

The deep, luminous blue of Crater Lake is unbelievable —literally. When Kodak first began processing photographs of the lake, they apologized to customers because Kodak technicians felt sure that the unreal color of the lake in the photos must have resulted from a processing mistake. Actually, that famous blue stems from the lake's exceptional clarity and depth. As light passes through clear water, it gets absorbed color by color, with the reds going first and the blues last. Crater Lake is so deep—at 1,932 feet, among the deepest in the world—that every hue gets absorbed except for that radiant dark blue, which is scattered back to the surface for visitors to admire.

19

must be earned; the trail is 4 miles one way and the last mile or so entails scrambling up a steep scree slope and some hand-over-hand climbing.

Next, head due south to **Crater Lake National Park★ ★** *(541-594-2211)* and one of the world's most striking geological features. When you reach **Rim Drive★**, stop at the first viewpoint and take a gander at one of the most gorgeous lakes on earth and—at 1,932 feet—the deepest in the United States. On a sunny day the blueness of the water defies adjectives (see sidebar p. 19). The beauty of the water is enhanced by the setting; you admire the lake from the forested rim of a volcanic caldera, looming as much as 2,000 feet above the water's surface.

The 6-mile-diameter caldera formed some 7,700 years ago during a series of massive eruptions by Mount Mazama—the name given to the former mountain that now holds Crater Lake. To learn more, take a narrated **boat tour** *(541-830-8700. Late June–mid-Sept.; fare).* To reach the dock, you must hike the steep, mile-long **Cleetwood Trail,** worth the effort because it's the only way to get from the rim to the lakeshore. Make sure to feel the perpetually 38°F water.

Oregon countryside, near Klamath Falls

Tour, eat lunch, or stay at historic **Crater Lake Lodge** *(541-830-8700. Mid-May–mid-Oct.),* extensively renovated in the mid-1990s. The view of the lake from the lodge's balcony is unsurpassed. Stretch your legs along the hiking trails veining the thousands of acres of parkland, or take the **Castle Crest Wildflower Garden Trail,** a short, easy walk along a brook that flares with flowers in midsummer. The **Annie Creek Canyon Trail** offers a 1.7-mile loop through a deep canyon alive with wildflowers and wildlife.

To experience a very different body of water, drive south on Oreg. 62 and then US 97 to vast, shallow **Upper Klamath Lake.** This is part of a complex of lakes, creeks, marshes, meadows, forests, and grasslands comprising the **Klamath Basin,** which sprawls all the way into California. Although a large majority of these terrifically productive wetlands have been turned into farmland, much of the remainder has been somewhat protected as the **Klamath Basin National Wildlife Refuges** ★ *(916-667-2231).*

In peak years up to two million ducks and geese descend on the refuges during the spring and fall migrations, and in winter as many as a thousand bald eagles gather here. Hundreds of animal species call the basin home year-round. You're likely to spot some, particularly birds, from the road, but canoeing into the marshes is the best way to see wildlife and get a true feel for life in the tules. Try the **Upper Klamath Refuge Canoe Trail** *(Rocky Point Resort 541-356-2287. Rent canoes at launch site)* on the west side of Upper Klamath Lake. Huge white pelicans, water snakes, ospreys, river otters, and lots of waterfowl are seen regularly as you meander amid the cattails and lily pads.

Continue viewing wildlife at the town of **5** **Klamath Falls** *(Department of Tourism 541-884-0666 or 800-445-6728)* by walking the **Link River Nature Trail** or the **Wingwatchers Trail.** But natural history takes a backseat to human history in this town, which boasts three fine museums. The **Favell Museum of Western Art and Indian Artifacts** ★ *(125 W. Main St. 541-882-9996. Closed Sun.; adm. fee)* houses one of the largest and finest collections of Native American artifacts in the region—the arrowheads alone number 60,000 and include a radiant fire-opal point. The museum also displays the works of more than 300 Western artists.

The **Klamath County Museum** ★ *(1451 Main St. 541-883-4208. Closed Sun.; adm. fee)* casts its net even wider, starting with Native American artifacts from 10,000 years ago and detailing county history right up to modern times. Plenty of information brings the objects to life. The **Baldwin Hotel Museum** *(31 Main St. 541-883-4208. June-Sept. Tues.-Sat.; adm. fee),* a 1906 downtown landmark, recalls everyday life in early Klamath Falls through an idiosyncratic collection of artifacts, from a historic photography studio to old ice-cream cartons from the locally famed Crater Lake Dairy. From here, Oreg. 140 leads west over the mountains to Medford, completing the loop.

21

● 115 miles ● 1 to 2 days ● Spring through autumn

White-haired waves hurl themselves against rocky shores. Lush conifer forest hovers over a sandy beach. Fishing boats sway with the swell in small-town harbors. Seabirds swirl above offshore pinnacles. Lighthouses wink from rugged headlands. Welcome to a classic stretch of Oregon coast. To these definitive attributes add boat trips, hikes through a redwood forest, a boisterous colony of seals and sea lions, and the formal gardens of a historic estate.

The town of ❶ **Brookings** *(Chamber of Commerce 541-469-3181)* grew up at the mouth of the Chetco River. Its rich mix of maritime and pioneer history is recalled at the **Chetco Valley Museum** *(15461 Museum Rd. 541-469-6651. May-Sept. Wed.-Sun., Oct.-April Fri.-Sun.; adm. fee).* Ask about the iron casting of a woman's face, thought by some to be a likeness of Queen Elizabeth I left by Sir Francis Drake.

For a taste of the interior, head east to **Azalea Park** *(Left on Old County Rd. off Constitution Way. 541-469-2163),* a riot of blooming wild azaleas from April through June. Head east about 8 miles to ❷ **Alfred A. Loeb State Park** *(North Bank Chetco River Rd. 541-469-2021. Information about any state park on this drive can be obtained from the Oregon State Park Information Center in Portland. 800-551-6949).* Park beside the grove of old myrtlewood trees; as you continue up the coast you'll see many signs advertising products made from this uncommon and beautiful hardwood. Hikers should grab a keyed interpretive booklet and take the short (less than a mile) **Riverview Trail** along the Chetco. At trail's end, cross over the road and continue on the **Redwood Nature Trail ★,** a mile-long

Dahlias, Brookings

loop through a fine old-growth redwood forest. This is about as far north as redwoods occur naturally.

Just up US 101 from Brookings, motorists start into the 55 miles of what is arguably the Northwest's most scenic stretch of coastline. The most stunning section comes first, in the form of **Samuel H. Boardman State Scenic Corridor**★★ *(541-469-2021)*. This skinny shoreline preserve runs for about 13 miles and offers many hiking trails, beach picnic areas, and viewpoints. The trail from the **Indian Sands Viewpoint**★ leads to sand dunes on a slope well above the surf. Beyond the small dune area, a trail cuts through the dense coastal scrub on a steep mountainside high above the ocean to 345-foot ❸ **Thomas Creek Bridge,** the highest bridge in Oregon. A mile or two north of the bridge is the trail to **Natural Bridge Cove**★. Travelers can gaze upon this exquisite little cove from the viewpoint or take a short but steep trail through the Sitka spruce forest down to a level bench that overlooks both cove and open ocean.

Continue north to **Cape Sebastian State Scenic Corridor** *(541-469-2021)*, driving to the south lookout point for a 360-degree view. A trail leads out onto the cape for more vistas. Another few miles brings you to the only

23

Fishing boats, Brookings harbor

natural feature in the area that can compete with the coast: the **Rogue River**★. Several tour operators offer jet-boat rides, raft trips, and lodge-to-lodge hiking trips on this famed fishing river, much of which is designated wild and scenic *(see sidebar this page. For information, contact Chamber of Commerce, Gold Beach. 541-247-7526 or 800-525-2334).*

From the Rogue, this drive continues along the coast, alternately hugging the beach and scaling mountainsides high above the surf. Hike through an old-growth forest of 15-foot rhododendrons and 200-foot cedars to the tallest of those seaside mountains (1,756 feet) on the steep, 3-mile **Humbug Mountain Trail**★. Down near the trailhead, **Humbug Mountain State Park** *(541-332-6774)* comprises a picnic area, campground, and a small black-sand beach.

The 55-mile-shoreline run ends a few miles north in ❹ **Port Orford** *(Chamber of Commerce 541-332-8055)*, a small fishing and logging town blessed with dramatic ocean views. For the next 25 miles the highway stays inland, passing through woodlands and pastures. Travelers who can't part with the coast for even half an hour can turn off US 101 4 miles out of Port Orford and drive west to **Cape Blanco State Park** *(541-332-6774)*. The last stretch of the road winds through coastal forest and meadows and along the narrow, 200-foot-high headland to the Cape Blanco Lighthouse. This is the westernmost point in Oregon, and, as the stunted, twisted trees attest, it's also exposed to fierce storms; wind speeds of 184 miles per hour have been recorded here.

US 101 returns to the sea in the charming town of ❺ **Bandon**★ *(Chamber of Commerce 541-347-9616)*. Bandon's heart can be found in the pedestrian-friendly section called **Old Town**★ down by the harbor. Art galleries, a marina, a little history museum, cafés, a fish-packing plant with a retail outlet, a pier for fishing and crabbing, a dockside fish-and-chips joint, a driftwood museum: It's easy to spend hours poking around. But for ocean vistas that feature some striking sea stacks, head up onto the bluffs and drive south along Beach Loop Road as it follows shoreline cliffs to various beach access points in **Bandon State Natural Area** *(541-347-2209)*. North across the Coquille River from Old Town lies another popular seaside retreat, **Bullards Beach State Park** *(541-347-2209)*.

About 8 miles out of Bandon leave US 101 and cut left to the coast on West Beaver Hill Road. A few miles short of the shore on Seven Devils Road, stop at **South Slough National Estuarine Research Reserve**★ *(541-888-5558.*

Up the Rogue

Jet boats take tens of thousands of travelers up the Rogue River every year. The outfits that run these journeys offer two basic deals: a 64-mile or a 104-mile round-trip. Although the lower part of the river is lightly settled, it is still very pretty. Passengers will likely see herons, ducks, kingfishers, deer, and perhaps an eagle, a river otter, or a bear while listening to commentary on the river's natural and human history. The longer cruise penetrates the Wild Rogue Wilderness, motoring past 1,000-foot canyon walls and pristine conifer forest.

24

Reserve open daily. Interpretive Center closed Sat.-Sun. Labor Day–Mem. Day). Estuaries, where salt water from the sea mixes with freshwater from a river or creek, are among the richest places on earth, and this is an outstanding example of the kind found in the Northwest. Start at the Interpretive Center and peek at tiny estuary denizens through microscopes or large denizens through spotting scopes. The array of life is impressive, from ghost shrimp and algae to bears and ospreys. Several trails allow hikers to explore the reserve.

Continue on Seven Devils Road for a few miles and you'll hit the Cape Arago Highway in the little fishing village of **Charleston.** Turn southwest onto the highway for one last dose of the scenic south coast. **Sunset Bay State Park** *(541-888-4902),* a popular playground beach that offers picnicking and camping, is a 3-mile drive from town.

Just south lies **Shore Acres State Park★** *(541-888-3732. Fee).* The dramatically sculptured sandstone cliffs draw many onlookers, but its main attraction are the formal gardens, remnants of the grand estate of Louis J. Simpson, an early 20th-century tycoon. The mild climate means that flowers of some sort are blooming nearly every day of the year.

Stop at **Simpson Reef Overlook** to view the immense elephant seals and Steller's sea lions—males of these species weigh about two tons and one ton respectively—and the sleeker harbor

Cape Blanco Lighthouse

seals and California sea lions. Then continue to the highway's end at ⑥ **Cape Arago State Park★** *(541-888-4902).* From atop the bluffs visitors can see dozens of miles north and south along the coast; a few tables set in strategic positions provide some of the finest picnic sites in the state. It's noisy, though; not only do the waves keep crashing against the rocks, but during much of the year seals and sea lions bark incessantly from nearby offshore rocks, part of the Oregon Islands National Wildlife Refuge.

Central Coast and South

● 220 miles ● 2 to 3 days ● Spring through autumn

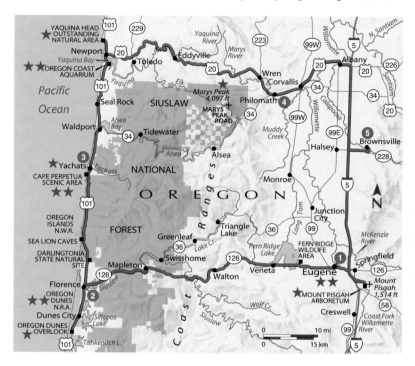

Long, uncrowded, undeveloped sandy beaches; wild rocky shores; mountains swathed in conifer forest; picturesque farms in a verdant valley; quiet little towns with a pioneer past; small, clean, livable cities—these are the attributes most often associated with Oregon, and this drive offers them all. It starts in Eugene, a university town and cultural center, then cuts west over the Coast Ranges to the beach. A trip to the south takes in the nation's most extensive coastal sand dunes before the route heads north along 50 miles of some of Oregon's finest coastline. At Newport the drive heads east back to the Willamette Valley and a few historic towns before returning to Eugene.

① **Eugene★★** *(Visitor Center 541-484-5307 or 800-547-5445)* is best known as the home of the Fighting Ducks, that is, the site of the **University of Oregon★** *(541-346-1000)*. Numerous historic buildings grace its grounds, including Villard Hall (1885) and Deady Hall (1876). For campus visitors who want to go back in time a little further, there's the **Museum of Natural History** *(1680 E. 15th Ave. 541-346-3024. Wed.-Sun.; donation),* which focuses on the state of Oregon with displays on local birds, native plants, and the region's geology. Best are the rooms devoted to native peoples. Visitors can gaze at 9,000-year-old sagebrush-bark sandals and 11,000-year-old spear points that might have been used to hunt mammoths.

On the west side of campus lies the handsome **Museum of Art**★ *(1430 Johnson Ln. 541-346-3027. Wed.-Sun.; donation).* Its collection ranges across the globe, but is particularly strong in Asian art. Trek up to the third-floor exhibit of Japanese dolls, fierce warriors, and horses definitely not for cuddling. Then relax in the charming courtyard amid a fountain, sculptures, and brick, colonnaded walkways.

Local history gets its due at the **Lane County Historical Museum** *(740 W. 13th Ave. 541-687-4239. Wed.-Sat.; adm. fee),* which details events up to the 1930s, including a "Jazz and Spats" exhibit on how locals behaved during the Roaring Twenties. But, inevitably, most of the museum is dedicated to pioneer times, especially the Oregon Trail.

Visitors can glimpse Eugene's out-of-the-mainstream soul at the **Fifth Street Public Market**★ *(296 E. 5th Ave. 541-484-0383).* Located in the oldest part of downtown, the market comprises dozens of shops and businesses in a cluster of rambling old brick buildings wrapped around a pretty courtyard. Especially revealing are the 15 eateries, with nary a chain restaurant in sight. There's a wide variety, including one deli that has a flat of wheat grass on its counter; workers snip off a few shoots to add to salads. Locals hang out in these cafés, reading the paper and watching the musicians, jugglers, and other performers who often show up.

Outdoor café, Fifth Street Public Market, Eugene

Eugene is rich in parks and green space, but the **Mount Pisgah Arboretum**★ *(34909 Frank Parrish Rd. 541-747-3817)* stands out in the crowd. Its 200 acres sprawl along the Coast Fork of the Willamette River, at the base of Mount Pisgah. Seven miles of trails take visitors along the river, through wetlands, and into forest. One leads to the 1,514-foot summit of Mount Pisgah and serves up expansive views of the Willamette Valley and the Cascades and Coast Ranges.

From Eugene the drive heads west on Oreg. 126 about 7 miles to **Fern Ridge Lake,** popular for boating, fishing,

Dunes

Rising hundreds of feet, the sand hills of the **Oregon Dunes National Recreation Area** are the nation's tallest coastal dunes. Countless sand grains erode from sea cliffs and coastal watersheds and tumble to the sea, where currents sweep the tiny rock particles along the shore. Tides and waves carry the sand onto the beach, providing the raw material for the sculptor of dunes, the wind. However, European beach grass planted in parts of the dunes in the 1930s has flourished and spread along the entire shoreline of the recreation area, catching sand grains being blown inland and forming a foredune up to 25 feet high. This waylays most of the sand that would normally replenish the big dunes, which continually lose sand as it blows farther inland. Unless managers find a way to feed the sand-starved dunes, they will become covered in vegetation over time.

windsurfing, canoeing, and other water sports. The marshes and woods around the lake also harbor beavers, deer, foxes, muskrats, and some 250 species of birds. Wildlife-watchers should head for the **Fern Ridge Wildlife Area** *(Off Oreg. 126. 541-935-2591. Call for seasonal restrictions)* and hike the **Coyote Creek Nature Trail.**

Oreg. 126 continues west, climbing up the forested slopes of the Coast Ranges and at **Mapleton,** joining up with the **Siuslaw River** and flowing down to the coast at ❷ **Florence** *(Chamber of Commerce 541-997-3128)*. Take US 101 south half a mile and dip into **Old Town,** a pedestrian-friendly jumble of shops, galleries, and antique stores along the Siuslaw's estuary. Try some clam chowder at **Mo's** *(541-997-2185)* on the dock.

Then continue south on US 101 across the historic bridge to the **Oregon Dunes National Recreation Area**★★ *(Siuslaw National Forest 541-271-3611. Fee)*. This strip of forest, lakes, and enormous sand dunes stretches 40 miles down the coast, but you can see a fine sample if you drive about 9 miles down US 101 to the **Oregon Dunes Overlook**★. An observation platform provides a panoramic view of dunes, tree islands, wetlands, and the ocean, or hike out into this otherworldly landscape on a marked trail and feel the sand between your toes.

From Florence the drive heads north on US 101. To see a botanical oddity, pull off at **Darlingtonia State Natural Site** *(541-997-3851)*. *Darlingtonia* is the scientific name for a species also known as the cobra lily. Troop along the boardwalk above the bogs favored by these plants and you'll see that they do indeed look like cobras poised to strike. They're also carnivorous—interpretive signs explain how *Darlingtonia* lures insects into its snake head, traps them, and digests them.

About 10 miles north of Florence, US 101 rejoins the coast in dramatic fashion, emerging from forest and dunes onto steep bluffs high above the surf. A mile or so farther is **Sea Lion Caves** *(541-547-3111. Adm. fee)*, overly commercial, but interesting nonetheless. Cliff-top platforms yield grand vistas of the coast (and migrating gray whales mid-Feb. to mid-April and Nov.-Dec.), but the big draw is the boisterous Steller's sea lions seen out on the rock ledges or in a huge cavern reached by descending 208 feet via elevator.

The route clings to the coast as it goes north, sometimes tightroping high above the water, sometimes running right alongside the shore. After a dozen miles of sandy beaches, rocky points, and state parks, stop at **Cape Perpetua Scenic Area**★★ *(541-547-3289. Closed Mon.-Fri. Labor*

Oregon Dunes National Recreation Area

Day–Mem. Day; adm. fee).

The Interpretive Center contains some nice displays on the area's natural and cultural history, including a Discovery Cove for kids, but don't tarry too long because there's much to do outside. The several trails fall into two categories: shore and forest. Hikers with a hankering for big trees and a beautiful creek might try the 2-mile round-trip **Giant Spruce Trail**★.

Those raring to see the ocean would enjoy the half-mile-loop **Captain Cook Trail**★, which takes visitors down to a rugged rocky shore to explore tide pools and watch the waves blast the basalt. The steep **Cape Perpetua Trail**★ leads up the south face of the 803-foot cape that gave this scenic area its name. Or drive to the top of Cape Perpetua, the highest point in Oregon directly on the shore, for incredible views of the coast and the Coast Ranges.

Sea Lion Caves, north of Florence

A 3-mile drive north of the cape leads to the delightful little town of ❸ **Yachats**★ *(Visitor Center 541-547-3530),* where the **Yachats River** meets the sea. When the tide is out, there's a broad sandy beach and some tide pools at the mouth of the river. When the tide is in, you can walk along the ocean's edge and watch the waves attack the deeply incised rocky shore. The town itself is a pleasing blend of galleries, eateries, shops, and bed-and-breakfasts.

Twenty-five miles north lies the larger small town of **Newport** *(Chamber of Commerce 541-265-8801 or 800-262-7844),* situated on the larger **Yaquina River.** Side by side on the south shore of Yaquina Bay are Oregon's two leading institutions for teaching the general public about the sea: the **Oregon Coast Aquarium** ★ ★ *(2820 S.E. Ferry Slip Rd. 541-867-3474. Adm. fee)* and the **Hatfield Marine Science Center** ★ ★ *(541-867-0100. Closed Tues.-Wed. Labor Day–Mem. Day; donation).*

Between 1996 and 1998, "Where's Keiko?" were the first words of just about every kid who visited the aquarium. Although the killer whale star of the movie *Free Willy* no longer lives here (see sidebar p. 31), the aquarium has much to offer. For example, watching the slow, rhythmic pulsings of the moon jellies is positively hypnotic. Or go eyeball to eyeball with a wolf eel, guaranteed to send shivers down the strongest spine. And who doesn't smile at the antics of the sea otters in their big

Oregon coastline along US 101

Seagull, Yachats

outdoor pool? One exhibit allows visitors to guide a remote TV camera for close-up shots of their favorite tide-pool creatures. Another, opening in June 2000 in Keiko's old tank, comprises an acrylic tunnel from which visitors view three ocean habitats. And then there are the seabird aviary, the coast lab, the wetlands—more than enough to make this a half-day venture.

Across the way at the Hatfield Marine Science Center—Oregon State University's marine research facility—a renovated public wing opened in 1997. Designed to complement the aquarium, it makes current marine research topics accessible to the public. One exhibit shows how scientists track migrating whales by satellite, another tells about mapping the sounds of underwater volcanoes and earthquakes. Many displays engage visitors actively, such as the sea cave that kids can enter, and the touch tank that allows people to gently handle tide-pool dwellers.

Across the bay from the aquarium and marine science center sits Newport's **Historic Bayfront★**. It's an attractive blend of working waterfront (fishing boats, marine supply stores, fish-packing plant) and tourist center, with whale-watching trips, cafés, galleries, and the like.

Just off US 101 on the north side of Newport is the **Yaquina Head Outstanding Natural Area★** *(Bureau of Land Management 541-265-2863)*. Perched on the tip of this rugged headland is the **Yaquina Head Lighthouse,** the tallest and second oldest (1872) lighthouse in the state. Close offshore rise sea stacks on which nest thousands of murres and gulls and a few puffins, cormorants, and black oystercatchers. Stairs lead down the bluff to rich tide pools, where a Bureau of Land Management naturalist is often on hand to share his or her knowledge of the sea stars, urchins, hermit crabs, and other residents.

From Newport take US 20 across the Coast Ranges. On the east side, just west of ❹ **Philomath,** take a worthwhile side trip south on Oreg. 34 about 10 miles to Marys Peak Road. This road winds slowly to the 4,097-foot summit of **Marys Peak★**. From the meadows at the top visitors can see the Pacific Ocean, the Cascades, the Willamette Valley, and even far to the north to Mount St. Helens and Mount Rainier in Washington. Trails lead through some old-growth forest near the summit.

31

Free Keiko

After the movie *Free Willy* came out in 1993, the American public clamored for its star, Keiko the killer whale, to be freed from an inadequate facility in Mexico. However, veterinarians determined that Keiko wasn't ready to survive in the wild, so the Oregon Coast Aquarium and the Free Willy Keiko Foundation built a spacious tank and flew the orca to his new home in 1996. His health improved steadily at the aquarium, and in September 1998 Keiko was flown to Iceland. He lives in a floating pen in the ocean where trainers teach him survival skills in the hope that one day Keiko can return to life in the wild.

Annual da Vinci Days, OSU

East of Philomath, US 20 enters the **Willamette Valley,** where oak-studded hills start replacing the conifer-clad mountains. In **Corvallis,** home of Oregon State University, US 20 bumps into the Willamette River, which it follows through farmlands northeast to **Albany** *(Visitors Association, 300 Second Ave. S.W. 541-928-0911 or 800-526-2256).* This small city of about 35,000 flourished as a river port and railroad center during the last half of the 19th century, creating an impressive legacy of more than 350 historic houses of many different styles. Get a map from the Visitors Association and stroll the historic districts. Among the homes open to the public is **Monteith House** *(518 Second Ave. S.W. 541-928-0911. Mid-June–mid-Sept. Wed.-Sun. and by appt.; donation),* the oldest (1849) pioneer frame house in town. More of Albany's history unfolds at the **Albany Regional Museum** *(302 Ferry St. S.W. 541-967-6540. June-Aug. Tues.-Sat., Sept.-May Wed. and Sat.).* Travelers still in a mood to commune with the past may also want to drive the back roads east of Albany, where eight covered bridges remain amid the farm fields.

A small-town version of a historic, Willamette Valley river-and-railroad town can be explored by heading down I-5 to Oreg. 228 and going east about 4 miles to ❺ **Brownsville** *(Chamber of Commerce 541-466-3390).* The town's settlement in 1846, the arrival of the woolen mill in 1862, the coming of the railroad shortly afterward—such historical milestones are covered at the **Linn County Historical Museum** *(101 Park Ave. 541-466-3390. Donation),* which also features a Contestoga wagon.

Brownsville's elegant past is recalled at the **Moyer House** *(204 N. Main St. 541-466-3070. Sat.-Sun.; donation),* an 1881 Italianate residence with bay windows, marble fireplaces, and stenciled ceilings.

From Brownsville, return to I-5 and drive south back to Eugene.

32

Unity Bridge, Lowell

Central Oregon

● 220 miles ● 2 to 3 days ● Late spring through autumn ● Cascade Lakes Hwy. may close in winter.

East meets west in central Oregon. This drive begins in Bend, with the Cascade Range to the west and the high desert to the east. The route moves in a crooked figure eight from sagebrush-grasslands to dry ponderosa pine woods, to the dense conifer forests of the mountains and back toward the high desert. Inviting stops along the way include a haute cowboy town, a spectacular river gorge, an outstanding desert museum, a national monument dedicated to volcanic features, and many appealing lakes and rivers.

❶ **Bend** *(Visitor Center 541-389-8799 or 800-800-8334)* serves as the hub of central Oregon and of this drive. The pretty town is also a gateway to the region's many recreational opportunities. To fully appreciate Bend's location, take Greenwood Avenue east to **Pilot Butte** *(Pilot Butte State Park 541-328-8160. Limited access in winter)*, which offers great views of the Cascades and the surrounding countryside.

Start sampling the region's delights by heading northwest on US 20 to ❷ **Sisters**★ *(Chamber of Commerce 541-549-0251)*. To vividly grasp the origin of the town's name, drive a mile west of town on Oreg. 242 to the Patterson Ranch *(Open to prospective customers only)* and look southwest; those looming, 10,000-foot-plus, snow-topped volcanoes are the **Three Sisters.** While at this vantage point, also take note of the scores of Rocky Mountain elk and 200 to 250 llamas grazing in the pastures before you.

Downtown Sisters is in the latter stages of transition from ranch town to tourist town. The wooden boardwalks are trod by more sport sandals than cowboy boots, and the Old West-style storefronts house more galleries than feed stores. One extreme example is **Antler Arts** *(210 E. Cascade St. 541-549-4251. Closed Sat.)*, for those who see antlers as the answer to all their decorating needs. Then check out **Soda Creek Gallery** *(178 S. Elm St. 541-549-0600. Closed Thurs. Nov.-May)*, **Folk Arts and Company** *(183 E. Hood Ave. 541-549-9556)*, and **Mountain Man Trading Post and Gallery** *(290 W. Cascade St. 541-549-1506)*, which sell a wide range of appealing goods, from guns to artwork.

Next, drive northwest along US 20/Oreg. 126 for about 5 miles to the turnoff for Indian Ford Campground and Forest Road 11 *(Sisters Ranger District 541-549-2111. Closed weekends)*. Take FR 11 north around the base of **Black Butte** and deep into a ponderosa pine forest characteristic of much of the east side of the Cascades. After about 10 miles the road turns to gravel, but decent gravel, sometimes rising several hundred feet above the heavily treed canyon as it winds along **Fly Creek.** After about 10 more miles, FR 11 ends at a crossroads. Take FR 1170 east for about 5 miles, watching the landscape as it begins turning from forest to steppe, then take a right on County Road 64 to ❸ **The Cove Palisades State Park**★ *(541-546-3412. Adm. fee)*. This 4,130-acre park centers around **Lake Billy Chinook,** a reservoir framed by dramatic basalt cliffs and surrounded by hills covered with sagebrush and junipers.

Head north on Mountain View Drive, which skirts the lake's eastern flank. Many fine viewpoints line the road, including one from which you can see ten of the Cascades' most prominent peaks. About 6 miles north sits **Round Butte Dam** *(541-475-1300. Observatory closed in winter)*, which can be viewed from an observatory 250 feet above it. Just 2 miles north, turn east onto Belmont Lane and go about a mile to Elk Drive. Take this north through canyon country to **Lake Simtustus** and **Pelton Dam,** and on to US 26 and a 3-mile trip to **The Museum at Warm Springs**★ *(2189 US 26. 541-553-3331. Adm. fee)*. Located on the vast **Warm Springs Indian Reservation,** this large, handsome, stone-and-wood museum introduces visitors to the history and culture of the Wasco, Paiute, and Warm Springs peoples: the three tribes that compose the Confederation of

Oregon desert flowers

34

Warm Springs Indians. In addition to outstanding artifacts, the museum tells its story through videotapes of ceremonies, audio tapes of each tribe's language, and a wonderful song chamber, in which visitors hear traditional songs while seeing videos of the land, the wildlife, and the singers.

Head back down US 26 to Madras, then go south on US 97 about 15 miles to the **Peter Skene Ogden Scenic State Viewpoint.** At first this appears to be nothing more

Crooked River, Smith Rock State Park

than a pleasant rest stop with a few informational signs, but walk to the retaining wall and look down; the sheer drop to the **Crooked River** 300 feet below will make your head spin. Hawks and vultures ride thermals rising along dark gorge walls, swallows knife through the air, and the descending trills of canyon wrens echo off the rock.

You can get down to the river and hike along its bright waters amid the lofty pinnacles of another rugged canyon at ❹ **Smith Rock State Park**★ *(3 miles E of Terrebonne. 541-548-7501. Adm. fee).* Those pinnacles and some hulking, orange-red rock faces offer some of the nation's most popular and challenging rock climbing; several vantage points allow you to watch the lycra-clad climbers make their ascents.

To view rocks of a different sort, continue on US 97 to **Redmond,** exiting at Yew Avenue. Turn left onto Canal Boulevard (which becomes the old Redmond-Bend

Highway) and proceed some 5 miles to McVey Avenue. From there follow signs to **Petersen Rock Gardens**★ *(7930 S.W. 77th St. 541-382-5574. Adm. fee).* This cheerfully eccentric place feels like a roadside attraction, but a classy one. Starting in 1935, a Danish immigrant farmer named Rasmus Petersen spent his next 17 years of spare time building things out of agate, petrified wood, lava, obsidian, jasper, and other rocks. His legacy is a 4-acre garden festooned with stone creations, such as ponds, castles, tables, bridges, miniature churches, and more.

River Otter, High Desert Museum, near Bend

Back on US 97, drive past Bend to the ❺ **High Desert Museum**★★ *(59800 S. US 97. 541-382-4754. Adm. fee).* Those who think of the eastern Oregon desert as a natural and cultural wasteland will know better by the time they leave this superb facility. A slow walk among the elaborate dioramas reveals that the human culture of this region has been developing for at least 8,000 years. You'll see re-creations of a prehistoric Indian site, a fur trapper's camp, and a frontier town. Adjacent galleries display many more Indian and pioneer art and artifacts, and natural history exhibits feature trout, rattlesnakes, bats, lizards, and many other animals and plants that belie the desert's reputation for barrenness. That image further dissolves outside in the museum's 20 acres of zoolike exhibits, which include a birds of prey center, a river otter pond, and a porcupine habitat.

About 5 miles south, a 500-foot cinder cone rises on the west side of the highway. That's **Lava Butte**★ and its presence indicates that you've entered **Newberry National Volcanic Monument**★★. Turn into the **Lava Lands Visitor Center**★ *(58201 S. US 97. 541-593-2421. May–mid-Oct.; adm. fee. Shuttle bus from center to summit Mem. Day–Labor Day; fare)* and start learning about central Oregon's prolific volcanic past—and future. After browsing the interpretive displays, step outside to a trail that winds through a small part of the 9 square miles of hardened lava that flowed out of Lava Butte some 6,000 years ago. To see the source of all that lava, walk up the trail to the foot of the cinder cone, where lava breached the thinner south side of the butte. Follow the road to the **Crater Rim Trail,** which provides great views of the crater and of the area. Another volcanic feature, **Lava River Cave** *(Adm. fee),* lies a mile south of the center. Bring warm clothing and two light sources (lanterns may be rented) to explore this mile-long lava tube.

Big Obsidian Flow★

About 1,300 years ago Newberry Volcano erupted, pumping out gooey waves of lava rich in silica and laced with iron oxide. This is the recipe for obsidian, and the lava hardened into the **Big Obsidian Flow** *(Southern section of Newberry National Volcanic Monument. 541-593-2421. Limited access mid-Nov.–mid-May; adm. fee),* a square mile of obsidian up to 300 feet thick. Indians traded this high-quality obsidian throughout the Northwest, where it was prized by makers of arrowheads, knives, and other sharp tools. Because obsidian blades are sharper than steel, some modern-day doctors use them for delicate operations. You can explore the flow via a 0.75-mile trail.

Proceed south on US 97 for about 3 miles and turn west onto South Century Drive, the start of what used to be the Century Drive, when it was 100 miles long. Road improvements shortened it to 87 miles, and it was renamed the **Cascade Lakes Highway**★★ *(Visitor Center 541-389-8794 or 800-800-8334. Road closed in winter).* However, the drive's beauty and variety remain undiminished. Follow it past the resort community of **Sunriver** to FR 42, which travels across the Little Deschutes River and through a young ponderosa pine forest to FR 46. Take this north for some 3 miles to the turnoff for ❻ **Osprey Observation Point**★ on **Crane Prairie Reservoir.** A short trail leads from the parking lot to the observation area on the reservoir's western shore, where migrating osprey hang out from May to October. Observers may see these big birds of prey plunging talons-first into the water after fish. Bald eagles, river otters, sandhill cranes, and other wildlife also inhabit the area.

FR 46 continues north, flirting with the Deschutes River until it passes **Little Lava Lake,** the headwater of the Deschutes, and **Lava Lake.** A few miles later, **Elk Lake** offers many recreational opportunities, including swimming and sailing. By now the ponderosas have given way to a forest of mixed conifer through which you can glimpse great views of **Mount Bachelor,** its broad, 9,065-foot-high bulk just 5 miles to the east.

As the drive bends back toward Bend, park at **Devils Lake Campground** *(Fee)* and walk east a short distance to the small mountain of lava boulders known as **Devils Hill.** A piece of volcanic rock from this hill lies on the moon, placed there by Apollo astronauts who trained in these lava fields while preparing for lunar landings. Just below Devils Hill is a lovely enclave known as ❼ **Devils Garden**★, where several springs have created a small meadow sprinkled with wildflowers and shot through by little ponds and rivulets.

Continue east on FR 46, past lakes, forest, trailheads, and a small pumice desert. The highway turns into Oreg. 372 as it approaches the **Mount Bachelor Ski and Summer Resort**★ *(541-382-2607. Lift fee).* This is one of Oregon's major ski areas, but in summer you can ride to the summit, where views and naturalists await. From here, drive east on Oreg. 372 back to Bend.

Lava River Cave, Newberry National Volcanic Monument

● **175 miles** ● **2 to 3 days** ● **Spring through autumn**

In the 1840s, pioneers forded rivers, labored over mountains, and trudged across vast deserts as they followed the Oregon Trail to the promised land: the Willamette Valley. This drive lets late 20th-century travelers see what has become of the fabled valley that drew settlers across the continent. The route starts in Portland, where a sophisticated city has replaced the wilderness, and proceeds to the historical riches of Oregon City, the end of the Oregon Trail. The drive then winds south through farmlands and forests to one of Oregon's premier flower-producing areas, where you can stop and smell the roses, to a state park renowned for its waterfalls. After a look at history and current affairs in Salem, Oregon's capital, the drive swings back to Portland via the valley's wine country.

In 1845 the 640-acre wilderness clearing that became modern ❶ **Portland**★★ *(Visitor Center 503-222-2223 or 800-345-3214)* cost 25 cents, and that was the filing fee. Today Portland is a city of almost half a million people in a metropolitan area of some 1.6 million, and skyscrapers have sprouted amid the trees and wildflowers. The modern city hasn't completely erased the past, however. A bit of wilderness lives on in the large **Forest Park**★★ *(503-823-2223),* where some 50 miles of trails crisscross 5,000 acres of forested hills. Instead of the pigeons that one typically associates with city parks, elk, black bears, and bobcats roam. Evidence of Portland's human past remains in the form of many historic buildings, notably in the **Skidmore/Old Town Historic District** *(Between the North Park Blocks and Williamette River, S of Union Station).*

Visitors can learn more about the state at the **Oregon History Center**★ *(1200 S.W. Park Ave. 503-222-1741. Closed*

Mon.; adm. fee). The Portland exhibit steals the show with
engaging details about the city's early days. There's even a
"Benson Bubbler": one of the many bronze drinking fountains placed around town in the early 1900s
by timber baron Simon Benson to encourage
his workers to eschew alcoholic beverages.

Among the dozens of other Portland
museums are a children's museum, a police
museum, an advertising museum, and a
UFO museum. The **Portland Art Museum**★
*(1219 S.W. Park Ave. 503-226-2811. Closed Mon.;
adm. fee)* is noted for its modern paintings;
sculpture; English silver; and Native American, Asian, and pre-Columbian art. The **Pit-**

Pittock Mansion, Portland

tock Mansion★ *(3229 N.W. Pittock Dr. 503-823-3623. Adm.
fee)* is 16,000 square feet of French Renaissance splendor
set atop a hill overlooking the city, but it isn't just a gaudy
tribute to some rich guy's ego. Constructed in 1914 by Oregon Trail pioneer and newspaper publisher Henry Pittock,
it was built by Northwest craftsmen using Northwest materials in an effort to promote the region's virtues.

39

More contemporary matters come to light in the spacious **Oregon Museum of Science and Industry**★★

Riverplace café alongside the Willamette River, Portland

(1945 S.E. Water Ave. 503-797-4000. Adm. fee), one of the
nation's largest science museums. Brave the earthquake
room and get rattled by a 5.5 temblor. Touch a tornado.
Beam a message into outer space. Check out the

Metro Washington Park Zoo, Portland

planetarium, laser shows, and OMNI-MAX theater. Board the U.S.S. *Blueback,* the Navy sub used in the movie *The Hunt for Red October.* You can spend the better part of a day here.

Another Portland institution that caters to knowledge-hungry citizens is **Powell's City of Books**★★ *(1005 W. Burnside St. 503-228-4651 or 800-878-7323),* the largest new and used bookstore in the United States. It occupies an entire city block and holds more than a million volumes; the staff hands out maps to help you navigate. But don't be misled by its size. Powell's emphatically is not a chain megastore. It's an independent loaded with idiosyncratic charm and stocked with books carefully selected for quality, not just for salability. Visit the rare book room, a venerable nook that evokes a private 19th-century library. Grab a bite at the café, a hangout for Portlanders from Gen-Xers to AARP members. Sit by the big windows in the second floor's northeast corner and let your book and the views compete for your attention. And resign yourself to the fact that you'll emerge from Powell's lugging a sack of books.

Beyond Portland's core lie many appealing sites, but one stands out: **Washington Park**★★ *(503-823-2223),* where many of Portland's leading attractions are clustered. In recent years, the **Metro Washington Park Zoo**★★ *(4001 S.W. Canyon Rd. 503-226-1561. Adm. fee)* has replaced many of its cages with spacious, naturalistic habitats that make both animals and zoogoers happier. Wander through the misty West African rain forest, the Alaskan tundra, and the Penguinarium, where dozens of endangered Humboldt penguins live in an award-winning exhibit that simulates their native Peruvian coastal habitat—a wave machine and Jacuzzi-like jets even mimic ocean currents.

Across the parking lot from the zoo is the **World Forestry Center**★ *(503-228-1367. Adm. fee),* a natural for Oregon, one of the world's great forest regions. One exhibit examines the controversy over the logging of old-growth forests. Other displays have examined the biology of trees, fighting forest fires, and tropical rain forests.

Washington Park also holds three notable gardens. The **Japanese Garden**★ *(611 S.W. Kingston Ave. 503-223-1321. Adm. fee)* is a tranquil oasis of ponds, graceful little bridges, cherry trees, and carefully placed stones. In 1988 Japan's ambassador to the U.S. called this the most authentic

Weather Machine

40

Tourists often join locals at noon in **Pioneer Courthouse Square** *(Yamhill and Sixth Ave.)* for a Portland ritual: watching the Weather Machine. Through most of the day this kinetic sculpture appears as a silver ball at the top of a mast, but at 12 o'clock, amid a fanfare of trumpets, three figures emerge in succession: a dragon, a great blue heron, and a sun goddess. The dragon symbolizes storms and heavy rain, the heron stands for overcast skies and drizzle, and the goddess promises sunshine. After the opening procession, one of the figures reemerges; it constitutes that day's weather prediction.

garden of its kind outside Japan. Ten miles of trails wind through **Hoyt Arboretum**★ *(4000 S.W. Fairview Blvd. 503-823-3654)*, especially renowned for its large variety of conifer species. The **International Rose Test Garden**★ *(400 S.W. Kingston Ave. 503-823-3636)* is the oldest and one of the largest rose test gardens in the country. The blossoms peak in late June, but with more than 530 varieties and more than 8,000 rose bushes, visitors can stop and smell the roses in other months too. And when all the petals have dropped, you've always got the elevated view of Portland with Mount Hood rearing up in the background.

Pioneers traveled 2,000 miles on foot and in wagons to reach the end of the Oregon Trail in ❷ **Oregon City**★ *(Chamber of Commerce 503-656-1619 or 800-424-3002)*. From central Portland you'll only have to drive 15 miles down Oreg. 99 E to reach the first incorporated American city (1844) west of the Mississippi. Not surprisingly, history occupies center stage here, starting with the three 50-foot-high covered-wagon-shaped buildings of the **End of the Oregon Trail Interpretive Center**★ *(1726 Washington St. 503-657-9336. Adm. fee)*. Rather than merely display artifacts, the center tries to convey life on the trail through living history presentations by guides in period dress.

More traditional exhibits on the Oregon Trail and the frontier days in the Willamette Valley can be found at the **Clackamas County Museum of History** *(211 Tumwater Dr. 503-655-5574. Adm. fee)*. From its site overlooking the Willamette River, visitors get a fine view of broad, 40-foot-high **Willamette Falls.** Many historic buildings sprinkle the old

On the Willamette River near Oregon City

part of town near the river and on the bluffs above, including the **McLoughlin House National Historic Site** *(713 Center St. 503-656-5146. Closed Mon. and Jan.; adm. fee)*. Dr. John McLoughlin built this Georgian Revival home in 1845, after retiring from the Hudson's Bay Company. Though a Canadian-born British subject who started out trying to claim Oregon for Great Britain, McLoughlin ended up supporting American settlers, earning himself the nickname "Father of Oregon."

Heading south on Oreg. 213, the surroundings soon shift from urban to rural. Drive about 30 miles through the green farmlands that pioneers dreamed of long ago to the little town of ❸ **Silverton** *(Chamber of Commerce, 421 S. Water St. 503-873-5615. Walking tour map available),* where you can stretch your legs by strolling through the historic downtown or crossing Silver Creek to meander through some quiet neighborhoods peppered with venerable old houses, notably craftsman-style bungalows. The chamber provides a tour map that lays out several loop drives through the surrounding countryside, which features berry farms, hop fields, a winery, a pioneer cemetery, Christmas tree farms, and a covered bridge. Just southwest of town sprawls one of the world's largest iris producers, **Cooley's Gardens**★ *(11553 Silverton Rd. N.E. 503-873-5463. Mid-May–early June).* Drive by the millions of irises in Cooley's fields or walk through the elaborate display garden, showcasing hundreds of varieties, often with wacky names, such as moomba, rustler, and Taco Supreme. Garden lovers should also watch for the coming of **Oregon Garden,** scheduled to open in 2000, with a partial opening slated for 1998.

To trade pastoral for wild and farm for forest, follow Silver Creek and Oreg. 214 southeast to ❹ **Silver Falls State Park**★ *(503-873-8681. Adm. fee).* A number of hiking, biking, and equestrian trails lace Oregon's largest state park (8,700 acres), but the hands-down winner is the **Trail of Ten Falls**★★. It snakes 7 miles along heavily forested Silver Creek from one waterfall to another—and even behind three of the cascades. The highest rains down from 177 feet. Hikers can start at either end of the trail or walk down to join it from one of the several overlooks above.

From Silver Falls, go west 15 miles on Oreg. 214, turn onto Oreg. 22, and drive another 10 miles to Oregon's capital city of ❺ **Salem**★ *(Visitor Center 503-581-4325 or 800-874-7012).* Logic dictates that visitors start a visit of Salem at the **State Capitol**★ *(900 Court St. N.E. 503-986-1388. Tours available).* Perhaps it's just as well that the first two capitol buildings burned down, as this 1938 neo-Grecian rendering of Vermont marble is a beauty. The rotunda and halls brim with murals, statues, paintings, and displays that depict key events and people from Oregon's past.

Salem's early history can be explored further at **Mission Mill Village**★ *(1313 Mill St. S.E. 503-585-7012. June-Sept.*

Children's Museum

The Gilbert House Children's Museum★ *(116 Marion St. N.E., Salem. 503-371-3631. Closed Mon. July-Feb.; adm. fee)* is housed in two historic Victorian homes on Salem's downtown riverfront, but its attitude is emphatically contemporary. Its hands-on exhibits touch on science, music, art, nature, and drama. This breadth reflects the Renaissance man who inspired the museum, Salem resident A.C. Gilbert (1884-1961), a highly successful businessman, an Olympic pole-vaulter, a world-class magician, and an inventor. His creations include the Erector set, American Flyer trains, and the predecessor of the Dust Buster. Kids can make bubble hoops in the bubble room, crawl amid a landfill in the recycling room, and drive adults insane in the karaoke room.

Thomas Kay Woolen Mill, Mission Mill Village, Salem

Tues.-Sun., Oct.-May Tues.-Sat.; adm. fee). You hear more than a figurative echo of the past when tour guides turn on the booming 1940s power loom in the cavernous 1896 **Thomas Kay Woolen Mill,** which occupies center stage in this 5-acre history complex. From sheep to shawl, visitors see the old ways of processing wool. The grounds also hold several historic buildings, a café, and the old mill race.

After contemplating the spartan living at Mission Mill Village, you'll appreciate the luxury of **Deepwood Estate** *(1116 Mission St. S.E. 503-363-1825. May-Sept. closed Sat., Oct.-April closed Tues. and Sat.; adm. fee).* This elaborate 1894 Queen Anne Victorian is a beautiful blend of gables, golden oak woodwork, exquisite stained-glass windows, and formal gardens. Across **Bush Park** from Deepwood— it makes a nice walk—stands another landmark: **Bush House** *(600 Mission St. S.E. 503-363-4714. Closed Mon.; adm. fee).* This 1878 Victorian mansion is considered as much a museum as a house because its structure and most of its furnishings are original and in fine condition. Experts come just to study the wallpaper. Also on the grounds is the **Bush Barn Art Center,** an artists' outlet.

From Salem, head north on Oreg. 221 along the west bank of the Willamette River, past Christmas tree farms, horse pastures (the area is known for its thoroughbreds), llama ranches, produce stands, oak and conifer wood-lands, vast hazelnut orchards (about 90 percent of the nation's crop comes from this region), fluffy knots of sheep, pick-your-own farms, and the little old Wheatland Ferry,

Château Benoit Winery, Lafayette

which carries six cars at a time across the Willamette. Convertibles and Sunday drives were made for such places.

Continue north on Oreg. 221 to Oreg. 18 and you'll be in the midst of **Willamette Valley wine country** *(Greater McMinnville Chamber of Commerce 503-472-6196).* Just before the junction lies the disheveled but historic town of **Dayton** *(Chamber of Commerce 503-864-2221),* which features an 1856 blockhouse, an 1880 Baptist church, and a pioneer cemetery. A few miles east lies a thicket of ten wineries, starting with **Sokol Blosser** *(Oreg. 99 W. 503-864-2282 or 800-582-6668).* Astride a hill, this small outfit offers views that reach clear to Mount Hood and a signed walk through a bit of vineyard where budding connoisseurs can learn to tell Pinot Noir grapes from Muscat Ottonels. In nearby ❻ **Lafayette** travelers can stop by the **Lafayette Schoolhouse Antique Mall** *(748 Oreg. 99 W. 503-864-2720),* where more than a hundred antique dealers hawk their wares in the former classrooms of a circa 1910 school. Seven miles southwest of McMinnville, on Oreg. 18, visitors can contemplate (and buy) the varied works of more than 200 Northwest artists at the **Lawrence Gallery** *(503-843-3633).* Next door is the **Oregon Wine Tasting Room** *(503-843-3787. Adm. fee refunded with purchase),* where one can sample a changing selection of Oregon wines and then choose a bottle from any one of the state's wine-producing regions.

From McMinnville head 25 miles north on Oreg. 47 to another wine country hub, ❼ **Forest Grove** *(Chamber of Commerce, 2417 Pacific Ave. 503-357-3006).* Its pleasant, historic downtown is home to **Pacific University** *(503-357-6151),* one of those small, tree-shaded liberal arts campuses that carries itself like a distinguished professor who's graying around the temples. Tuesday through Friday afternoons, stop by the museum in **Old College Hall;** built in 1850, it's the oldest continuously used educational building in the Northwest. Pick up a map and other information at the Chamber of Commerce and then cruise the lovely landscape to the north, south, and east, much of which is

44

covered by the **Wine Country Scenic Loop★**. Just south of town is vast **Montinore Vineyards★** *(3663 S.W. Dilley Rd. 503-359-5012. Tasting room April-Dec., and weekends Jan.-March. Grounds open daily)*, one of the valley's leading wineries. Admirers of the elegant Victorian house on the property would never guess that it was modeled from a Sears, Roebuck design in the early 1900s. Not far off is a winery of a different sort: **Momokawa Sake Brewery** *(820 Elm St., off Oreg. 47 bypass. 503-357-7056 or 800-550-SAKE. Mon.-Sat.)*. For a treat, visit the tasting room of the only Japanese rice wine brewery in the Northwest.

Ramble east on Oreg. 8 to Cornelius, then take the turnoff for the **Dutch Mill Herb Farm** *(6640 N.W. Marsh Rd. 503-357-0924. March-Dec. Wed.-Sat. and by appt.)*, where basil, lavender, and other aromatic wares scent the air. Wending southeast past Hillsboro, turn right on River Road to **Northwest Alpacas** *(11785 S.W. River Rd. 503-252-2227. Fri.-Sun.)*, where you can take a tour to learn more about these creatures. There's also a store stocked with downright sensuous alpaca sweaters, shawls, and scarves. Return to Farmington Road/Oreg. 208 and turn right, heading east to the 1912

45

Countryside near Lafayette

Jenkins Estate★ *(8005 S.W. Grabhorn Rd. 503-642-3855)*, now a public park. Its 68 acres include an elaborate house patterned after an English royal hunting lodge, extensive formal gardens, and semiwild woods laced by trails. Nearby are the subdivisions that signal the outer edge of Greater Portland's sprawl. At this point head back to Portland on Oreg. 8.

● **235 miles** ● **3 days** ● **Spring through autumn**

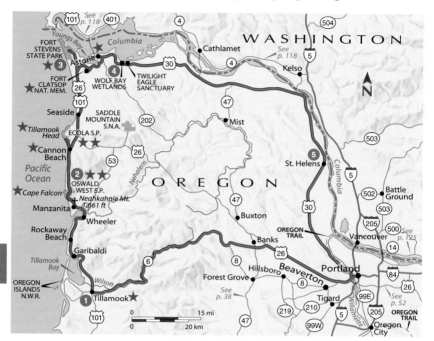

While Portland offers big-city amenities, and the road over the Coast Ranges and along the Columbia River takes in some pretty scenery and a few inviting historic towns, the coast defines this drive. Oregon's northernmost 65 miles of shoreline offer a multitude of pleasures, both natural and civilized. Visitors enjoy uncrowded sandy beaches and tony art galleries, lush coastal forests and sites where Oregon's modern history began, waves hammering rocky shores and a top-notch maritime museum. Those miles also include the unpredictable—an enormous cheese factory, an old blimp hangar that's now an aviation museum, and a winery that specializes in concoctions such as lemon meringue pie wine.

From Portland (see Willamette Valley drive, p. 38), head toward the sunset on US 26 and Oreg. 6, crossing the Coast Ranges along the Wilson River. When the alder and bigleaf maple give way to green pastures sprinkled with spotted cows, travelers know they're coming to ❶ **Tillamook**★ *(Chamber of Commerce 503-842-7525)*, famed for the tasty cheese produced by those dairy herds. Near the intersection of Oreg. 6 and US 101, plumb the history of the dairy industry and the region at the **Tillamook County Pioneer**

Museum *(2106 2nd St. 503-842-4553. Closed Mon. Oct.–mid-March; adm. fee)*. An enormous amount of stuff—more than 35,000 artifacts—is crammed into this former courthouse, including military gear, a stagecoach, a pump organ, a mounted bobcat, scary old medical equipment, and more than you'll ever see in one visit.

A much roomier attraction is located on the south side of town in a former blimp hangar, perhaps the world's largest wooden structure (1,072 feet long, 296 feet wide, and 192 feet high), that now houses the **Tillamook Naval Air Station Museum** *(6030 Hangar Rd. 503-842-1130. Adm. fee)*. Inside visitors can look over the large collection of World War II military aircraft, all operational and flown periodically during spring and summer.

Past and present come together on the north side of town just off US 101 at the **Latimer Quilt and Textile Center** *(2105 Wilson River Loop Rd. 503-842-8622. Closed Mon.; adm. fee)*. Displays of the traditional arts of quilting, spinning, basketry, needlepoint, and weaving are sometimes enlivened by the presence of local practitioners working at their arts.

Just north, travelers can answer Tillamook's most pressing question: Where does the milk from all those cows go? Most goes to the **Tillamook Cheese Factory**★★ *(4175 US 101 N. 503-842-4481)*. A dairy museum, video tour, and viewing deck well stocked with informational signs provide insight into the cheese-making process. Looking out at the vast jungle of stainless steel pipes and vats, visitors aren't surprised to learn that this factory produces about 50 million pounds of cheese a year. Needless to say, cheese samples are available, as well as Tillamook ice cream, more pertinent on a summer day.

Travelers get their first look at the coast a few miles north as US 101 hugs tightly to the water, following Tillamook Bay's contours up to the classic fishing

Cape Mears Lighthouse, near Tillamook

village of **Garibaldi** *(Chamber of Commerce 503-322-0301)*. While down at the pier, you might try some fishing, crabbing, or clamming. Those who prefer to fish with plastic can take home some of the ocean's bounty from **Miller's Seafood Market** or **Smith's Pacific Shrimp Company.**

From here, US 101 leaves the bay and strikes north

Short Sands Beach, Oswald West State Park

along the open Pacific. In the **Rockaway Beach** *(Chamber of Commerce 503-355-8108 or 800-331-5928)* area, a strip of seaside houses hides mile after mile of uncrowded sandy beach, reached via any number of access roads. About a mile north of Manzanita, **Neahkahnie Mountain Summit Trail**★ offers a chance to thoroughly stretch your legs. The fairly demanding trail leads up to a grand view of the coast and the valleys and mountains to the east. Actually, in this area the views from US 101 itself are noteworthy; the highway tightropes along the coastal mountainsides as high as 700 feet above the sea.

More outstanding hiking and views can be found just north of Neahkahnie Mountain at ❷ **Oswald West State Park**★★ *(503-368-5154 or 800-551-6949)*. From the parking lot, follow the easy trail down through a deep and dark spruce-hemlock forest to Smuggler Cove. Linger at this dramatic, rock-strewn beach (there's a campground and a picnic area) or take an hour to trek out to the tip of **Cape Falcon**★, where the forest peters out and hip-hugging paths lead through the scrub to 270-degree viewpoints.

Civilization returns in spades about 10 miles up US 101 in the form of **Cannon Beach**★ *(Chamber of Commerce 503-436-2623)*. This little beach town's fine expanse of sand is dominated by one of Oregon's most beloved landmarks, **Haystack Rock.** For years Cannon Beach was an overlooked artist's backwater, until tourism and money came to town. Visitors can now enjoy fine restaurants, art galleries galore, elegant bed-and-breakfasts, cute shops, and first-class resorts in a postcard setting. But during the high season it's hard to find a place to park, and many of the artists who made Cannon Beach's reputation now can't afford to live there.

Return to the wild coast by visiting Cannon Beach's neighbor to the north: **Ecola State Park**★★ *(503-436-2844 or 800-551-6949. Adm. fee)*. Drive a couple of miles into the park, stopping to stroll **Crescent Beach** or to lay out a picnic above Indian Beach. But the source of its

Saddle Mountain★

Standing above the other peaks in the Coast Ranges east of Cannon Beach and Seaside is 3,283-foot **Saddle Mountain** *(Saddle Mt. State Natural Area 503-368-5943. Limited access in winter)*. Hikers willing to huff and puff up the steep, 3-mile trail are rewarded with splendid views. However, Saddle Mountain's primary claim to fame lies at visitors' feet: the wildflowers. Between May and August wood lily, monkey flower, wild rose, pink coast fawn lily, and hundreds of other species bloom in the meadows and forest.

local renown is the hike over **Tillamook Head ★**. When the Lewis and Clark expedition camped nearby in 1806, and William Clark encountered Tillamook Head, he wrote, "I beheld the grandest and most pleasing prospect which my eyes ever surveyed." Visitors who ascend through the old-growth Sitka spruce forest to the 1,000-foot cliff where Clark stood (the place is marked) won't disagree.

US 101 returns to the sea 8 miles later in **Seaside** *(Chamber of Commerce 503-738-6391 or 800-444-6740)*. Seaside first began drawing tourists in the 1870s, and it remains an unabashed old-fashioned family beach resort. This is the place to stroll the promenade, barbecue hot dogs, roll along the sand in a "beachmobile," or munch on cotton candy while you're visiting the arcades.

About 10 miles north, US 26/101 reaches the end of its Oregon run and turns east, but travelers can continue a few miles to the extreme end of the coast at ❸ **Fort Stevens State Park ★** *(Ridge Rd. 503-861-2000. Adm. fee)*. In addition to trails, beaches, and a visible shipwreck, this state park lets visitors explore the former military facility that gave it its name. A museum and an extensive network

49

Cannon Beach from Ecola State Park

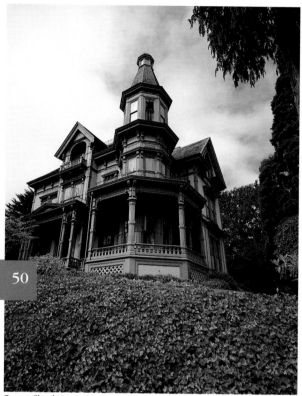

George Flavel House, Astoria

of old concrete bunkers tell the story of the artillery batteries that guarded the mouth of the Columbia from the Civil War until shortly after World War II.

Visit the site of an even older fort 5 miles southeast at **Fort Clatsop National Memorial**★ *(Fort Clatsop Rd. just S of U.S. Bus. 101. 503-861-2471. Adm. fee April-Sept.).* Visitors will be grateful for their hotels and motels after touring the re-creation of the crude and cramped stockade in which the Lewis and Clark expedition spent the winter of 1805-1806. The Visitor Center contains a small museum and in summer buckskin-clad interpreters demonstrate some of the skills that helped expedition members survive.

Across Youngs Bay lies one of the oldest permanent U.S. settlements west of the Mississippi: **Astoria**★ *(Chamber of Commerce 503-325-6311 or 800-875-6807).* Its location near the mouth of the mighty Columbia drew Lewis and Clark in 1805, fur traders in 1811, and later sailors and shipping magnates who made Astoria a thriving port. Three properties run by the Clatsop County Historical Society *(503-325-2203. Adm. fee good for all three sites)* recall Astoria's rich past: The **George Flavel House** *(441 8th St.)* is a splendid Queen Anne mansion built in 1885 by Captain George Flavel, a Columbia River bar pilot who kept an eye on river traffic from the fourth-story cupola. For a comprehensive look at the region's human and natural history, visit the jam-packed **Heritage Museum**★ *(1618 Exchange St.).* Fire-fighting equipment dating as far back as the 1880s and photos of historic Astoria fires highlight the **Uppertown Firefighters Museum** *(30th St. and Marine Dr. Fri.-Sun.).*

A study of Astoria's history wouldn't be complete without a trip to the **Columbia River Maritime Museum**★★

(1792 Marine Dr. 503-325-2323. Adm. fee). As a tour of this expansive museum reveals, sea and river are Astoria's heart and soul. Lurking amid the boats, models, paintings, and other artifacts are rousing tales of shipwrecks, whaling, and exploration. Outside at the museum's dock, visitors can board the *Columbia,* the last lightship (basically a seagoing lighthouse) to serve on the West Coast. Next door at the **17th Street Dock** visitors can tour two U.S. Coast Guard cutters *(503-325-6812 or 503-325-7213. Sun. by appt.)* when they're in port. Cruise ships occasionally dock there as well. Down a few blocks at the **14th Street River Park** *(503-325-5821),* interpretive displays on river and bar pilot operation include a radio speaker that lets visitors listen in on live conversations among boaters, pilots, and the Coast Guard.

For two overviews of Astoria and the area, head up 16th Street from the docks to the top of Coxcomb Hill and ascend 125-foot **Astoria Column** ★ *(503-325-2963).* As one would expect after spiraling up 164 stairs, the scenic overview from the top is spectacular. Equally impressive is the historical overview gained by examining the outside of the column. Created in 1926 and restored in 1995, pictorial friezes depicting key events in the area's history wrap around the column like one long mural.

The drive departs from the coast at Astoria and heads up the Columbia on US 30. About 6 miles along, take Old Highway 30 a short distance to the **Twilight Eagle Sanctuary.** Mount the viewing platform and scan for some of the bald eagles that haunt the ❹ **Wolf Bay Wetlands**—as many as 150 during the winter. Visitors can also read the interpretive signs on salt marsh ecology and look for other residents, such as terns, herons, and ducks.

Cruise for the next 60 miles or so through the green woods of the Coast Ranges, passing through a few small towns, some dairy lands, and occasionally glimpsing the Columbia out the driver's-side window. To visit the past and present of the lower Columbia, stop in ❺ **St. Helens** *(Chamber of Commerce 503-397-0685).* The historic downtown of this old river port is anchored by the **Columbia County Courthouse,** built in 1908 of locally quarried black basalt. In front of the courthouse is a pretty little town square and behind is **Columbia View Park,** which provides views of the landing, the fishing pier, a nearby houseboat community, river traffic, and Mount St. Helens rising in the distance.

From St. Helens it's a short run down US 30 back to the beginning of the drive, Portland.

Chocolate-Orange Wine?

A block from the Columbia River Maritime Museum in Astoria there's a place no self-respecting, rum-swilling old salt would be caught dead in: the **Shallon Winery** *(1598 Duane St. 503-325-5978. Open most afternoons).* Since the early 1980s, winemaker Paul van der Veldt has been concocting strange brews, such as chocolate-orange wine, a thick, brown mixture that almost prompts visitors to reach for a spoon. Other wines include cran du lait and lemon meringue pie. Van der Veldt creates these vintages as a labor of love, producing only about 500 gallons a year.

51

Zinnias, Sauvie Island Market, near Portland

Mount Hood Loop ★

● **160 miles** ● **2 to 3 days** ● **Spring through autumn**

Packing a suitcase for this drive is a pleasurable problem. Travelers may want presentable clothes, perhaps even evening wear, for the symphony, museums, and fine restaurants of Portland. But when the route heads to the wilds around Mount Hood, hiking boots, wool shirts, and ski outfits—even in summer—are de rigueur. Down in the Columbia River Gorge, you'll want casual clothes for visiting the fruit orchards, waterfalls, dam, and historic sites; and a wet suit for this windsurfing capital.

The drive starts in Portland (see Willamette Valley drive, p. 38), then heads east on US 26. By the time you pass through the hills near **Sandy,** about 20 miles out of Portland, the subdivisions and malls will have been replaced by farmlands. Another 5 miles east the rural setting gives way to forests of 150-foot Douglas-fir sprinkled with alder, cedar, and cottonwood.

Continue 14 miles to the ❶ **Mount Hood Information Center** (503-622-7674), which provides advice on everything from climbing the peak to huckleberry picking. The hiking and picnicking can begin just east in the pretty woods of the **Wildwood Recreation Site** (503-622-3696. Mid-May–mid-Oct.). Three miles east in **Zigzag,** travelers can turn north on Lolo Pass Road and take a 7-mile side trip to the **Ramona Falls**

Timberline Lodge lobby, Mount Hood

Trail. This popular path leads to cool Ramona Falls, where the **Sandy River** splits into a multitude of falling ribbons as it pours over a series of terraces. A short spur from Zigzag goes to the **Green Canyon Campground** *(Salmon River Rd. off US 26. 503-622-7674. Call for conditions),* where the **Old Salmon River Trail**★ winds through old-growth forest along the **Salmon River,** a designated wild and scenic river where you may see salmon spawning in season.

As you cruise farther on US 26, look around at the mountainous terrain and imagine crossing this chunk of the Cascades in 1846. That's the year Sam Barlow opened his toll road to serve as the last leg of the Oregon Trail. The Barlow Road largely ran along the same route as US 26,

Mount Hood rising beyond Oreg. 35 south of Hood River

but it was just a rough dirt track. As you whiz up the steep grade at **Laurel Hill,** about 8 miles east of Zigzag, picture pioneers straining at a rope wrapped around a tree, laboriously lowering their wagon down the mountainside.

Drive east on US 26 another five minutes—it would have taken the pioneers all day—and take the Timberline Road turnoff to ❷ **Timberline Lodge**★★ *(503-272-3311),* on the southern flank of **Mount Hood.** You'll have seen Oregon's highest mountain (11,239 feet) on and off since the beginning of the drive, but now it's time to get up close and personal by proceeding 6 miles north to the ski area at the end of the road.

Timberline is noted for its year-round skiing—access to some high slopes allows summer skiing. Ski-less summer visitors can ride the Magic Mile Chairlift *(fee)* up

Dams versus Salmon

The completion of the Bonneville Lock and Dam in 1938 marked the beginning of a four-decade dam-building boom on the Columbia River and its tributaries. Some dams, such as Grand Coulee, totally blocked salmon as they swam upriver to their spawning grounds or downriver to the ocean. Other dams installed fish ladders to help adults move upriver, but failed to assist juvenile salmon swimming downriver. Currently there are four migration options: through turbines, bypass systems, on barges and trucks, or over spillways. None are foolproof, and endangerment of salmon stocks continues. In addition to dams, overharvesting, change of habitat, and hatcheries have added to the decimation of the Columbia's legendary salmon runs. Evaluations and improvements continue as the Northwest tries to solve this thorny issue.

53

Farm east of Hood River

54

Hood River sidewalk café

to the 7,000-foot level for a grand view of Mount Hood and the Cascades. But Timberline is much more than a ski area. Climbers flock to Timberline to launch their assaults on the mountain; this perfect snow-cone peak attracts huge numbers of climbers each year. Hikers can find excellent trails at Timberline, including the 40-mile path that circles the mountain. Most of all, people come to see the lodge.

Dedicated in 1937 by Franklin Delano Roosevelt, Timberline Lodge was a flagship project of the Depression-era Works Progress Administration. The lodge was built on a grand scale to mirror the grandeur of the mountain. Ceilings soar dozens of feet overhead. The stone fireplace in the lobby is 92 feet around. The front stairway leads to a half-ton door, which opens onto a balcony with fine views of Mount Jefferson. Everywhere there is evidence of old-fashioned craftsmanship. The ripples on the massive timbers reveal that someone shaped them with broadax and adze. The andirons, light fixtures, and other ironwork are the creation of skilled blacksmiths. Newel posts shaped like owls and eagles are among the many hand-carved details that come out of the woodwork.

On US 26 a few miles past the Timberline Road turnoff, this drive turns north on Oreg. 35. Following the East Fork Hood River through 25 miles of mountains and forest, the highway enters the **Hood River Valley★,** a renowned fruit-growing area. Slow down and savor the vast pear, apple, cherry, and peach orchards. If it's springtime, feast on the sights and smells of the sea of blossoms. If it's summer or fall, ogle the fruit on the trees and watch the harvest. Browse the roadside stands and country stores, searching for old favorites, such as bing cherries and anjou pears, or exotic varieties such as winter banana apples and Flemish beauty pears. For a different perspective of

this idyllic valley, take the **Mount Hood Railroad**★ *(110 Railroad Ave. 541-386-3556 or 800-872-4661. April-Dec., call for hours; fare).* The four-hour, 44-mile round-trip ride on the historic train not only takes in the orchards but presents terrific views of Mount Hood and Mount Adams.

Oreg. 35 ends in ❸ **Hood River**★ *(Visitor Center, 405 Portway Ave. 541-386-2000 or 800-366-3530),* a town of about 4,500 on the Columbia River. Life in Hood River revolved around the orchards for decades (pick up a "Fruit Loop" map at the Visitor Center), but since the early 1980s another growth industry has heavily influenced the town: windsurfing, a.k.a. boardsailing. The outstanding conditions on the Columbia draw windsurfers from around the world. The demographics of boardheads can be deduced from Hood River's proliferation of espresso bars, upscale cafés, and shop windows featuring mannequins draped in garish wet suits. To watch boardsailors whisking across the water or to look into windsurfing for yourself, head down to the river at **Columbia Gorge Sail Park** (Call Visitor Center for more information).

Hood River marks this drive's entry into the **Columbia River Gorge National Scenic Area**★ ★ *(541-386-2333).* Drive west on I-84 and you'll soon be gazing up at the towering basalt cliffs on your side of the Columbia, and across the river to the forested mountains and verdant plateaus on the Washington side.

About 20 miles out of Hood River is **Cascade Locks** *(Visitor Center 541-374-8427. March-Nov.).* A hundred years ago, ships passed through here to evade the forbidding rapids. The completion of Bonneville Dam a few miles downriver (see sidebar p. 53) created a reservoir that buried the rapids, and put the locks out of business. The story of the locks

Windsurfing the Columbia River, near Hood River

and the area is explored at the **Cascade Locks Historical Museum** *(Cascade Locks Marine Park 541-374-8535. May-Sept.),* housed in the old lockkeeper's house. Also at the marine park is **Cascade Sternwheelers** *(503-223-3928. Mid-June–mid-Oct.; fare),* offering passage on a 145-foot copy of the stern-wheelers that used to ply the Columbia.

A few miles west, tour the huge structure that rendered the locks at Cascade Locks obsolete: ❹ **Bonneville Lock and Dam** *(541-374-8820)*. Dedicated in 1937, it was the first of the many federal dams that tamed the Columbia over the ensuing 40 years. Here travelers can watch locks that still operate, raising and lowering enormous barges.

To escape the car for one of the Columbia River Gorge's premier hikes, backtrack just east on I-84 and, after passing through a tunnel, take the first exit to the **Eagle Creek Recreation Area** *(541-386-2333. Call for trail conditions)* to hike the 13-mile **Eagle Creek Trail**★. It's steep in places and can be as long as hikers want to make it (after 13 miles it connects with the Pacific Crest National Scenic Trail at Wathum Lake), but many people go up just a few miles to sample the wildflowers, the narrow gorges sparkling with white water, the burly basalt outcroppings, and the waterfalls. About 6 miles up, the trail actually goes behind **Tunnel Falls.**

Some 6 miles west, experience the antithesis of an interstate: the **Historic Columbia River Highway**★★. The 17-mile-or-so stretch between here and Troutdale is the longest remaining portion of this scenic route, built between 1913 and 1917. Its purpose, in the words of its

Historic Columbia River Highway and the Columbia River Gorge

supervising engineer, Samuel Lancaster, was "to find the beauty spots, or those points where the most beautiful things along the line might be seen to the best advantage…." In addition, the slow, twisting road itself augments the beauty of the gorge with stone guardrails, arched bridges, rock walls, and lookout points that are testaments to the fine art of stonemasonry.

The land along the highway is loaded with waterfalls, lush forests, state parks, hiking trails, gorge overlooks, and picnic areas. About 3 miles from Warrendale is the **Oneonta Gorge**★, a split in the cliff that rises hundreds of feet overhead and averages about 20 feet across. In the summer, when Oneonta Creek is low, visitors willing to get their feet wet can hike a short way up this enchanting fissure to the waterfall at its end. Mosses, ferns,

Multnomah Falls, Columbia River Gorge National Scenic Area

57

and other plants that thrive on the gorge's perpetually cool, moist conditions thickly coat the basalt walls. Some are rare, and a few are unique to Oneonta Gorge, so the Forest Service has designated the gorge as a "special botanical area."

Multnomah Falls★, at 620 feet the highest waterfall in Oregon, does its cliff dive 2 miles west of Oneonta. A trail goes up to a bridge that spans the lower falls, and those with good knees can continue up steep switchbacks to a lookout above the falls. From Multnomah, the road passes one waterfall after another until it rises to the 733-foot promontory at ❺ **Crown Point State Scenic Corridor**★ *(503-695-2261)*. To capitalize on the point's grand views, the highway's builders erected **Vista House**★ *(503-695-2230. Mid-April–mid-Oct.),* which Lancaster called "an observatory from which the view both up and down the Columbia could be viewed in silent communion with the infinite." Inside are exhibits on the highway and the gorge. From here the route winds down to Troutdale, where it rejoins I-84 and returns to Portland.

North Central Backroads

● **230 miles** ● **2 days** ● **Spring through autumn**

Most motorists zipping through the Columbia River Gorge on I-84 don't realize that a slower, older Oregon sprawls to the south. This loop explores that quiet land, starting in The Dalles, an important historic town that was for many years the end of the land portion of the Oregon Trail. The drive proceeds through wheat country and ranch lands, where a great river offers fishing and white-water rafting. A semi-ghost town, several small but definitely living towns, rippling hills favored by pronghorn, and a national monument dedicated to fossils round out the route.

❶ The Dalles ★ *(Chamber of Commerce 541-296-2231 or 800-255-3385)* derived its name from the French-Canadian *dalle,* representing the kind of long, channeled rapids that made a nearby stretch of the Columbia treacherous to early *voyageurs* (those rapids are now buried beneath the reservoir created by The Dalles Dam). During America's westward migration, pioneers coming down the Oregon Trail faced a tough decision here: brave the rapids or face an arduous overland trek. Given The Dalles' pivotal

historical position, it's fitting that many fine 19th-century buildings remain. One of the oldest (1856) is the surgeon's quarters of old Fort Dalles, reborn as the **Fort Dalles Museum** *(500 W. 15th St. 541-296-4547. Call for hours; adm. fee)*. Inside the surprisingly elaborate military house and on the grounds are stagecoaches, a flintlock rifle collection, and other artifacts. Among the town's many gracious residences is the **Williams House Inn** *(608 W. 6th St. 541-296-2889)*, an exquisite 1899 Queen Anne, now a bed-and-breakfast.

The big news for history buffs is the long-anticipated opening (in May 1997) of the **Columbia Gorge Discovery Center**★ *(4500 Discovery Dr. 541-296-8600. Closed Mon.-Wed. mid-Nov.–mid-March; adm. fee)*. This extensive facility covers both the human and natural history of the Columbia River Gorge. On the same site are the **Wasco County Historical Museum,** a Native American longhouse, and more.

The modern era of The Dalles could be said to have begun in 1957 with the completion of **The Dalles Dam** *(Visitor Center, E edge of The Dalles. 541-296-1181. Call for tour train hours)*. After browsing the museumlike Visitor Center, take a small train to the dam for a guided tour. From here,

The Dalles Dam

the drive follows US 197 over the bluffs that border the Columbia and goes south across a high, semiarid plateau given to wheat farming. Those pioneers who chose the Barlow Road instead of the rapids followed much the same route back in the mid-1800s, heading for the **Tygh Valley,** where the overland trek climbed west over the Cascades.

From Tygh Valley an 8-mile trip goes east on Oreg. 216. About 5 miles along, turn off at the generic state park sign for **White River Falls State Park** *(541-739-2322)*. A grassy picnic area overlooks the broad, 90-foot-high series of waterfalls, and a trail leads down into the canyon below the pounding falls.

Badger, near Maupin

Three miles farther east, Oreg. 216 crosses the **Deschutes River** at **Sherar's Bridge.** Here the river screams through a long, narrow channel. In certain seasons, Native Americans mount the wooden platforms that hang over that frothing chute and use long-handled dip nets to fish for steelhead and salmon. The safety ropes around their waists indicate the riskiness of this age-old practice. White-water rafting—another somewhat risky venture—is also popular on the Deschutes. ❷ **Maupin** *(Chamber of Commerce 541-395-2599)*, south on US 197, is the center for many rafting outfits.

From Maupin, the drive continues 22 miles southeast on Bakeoven Road, then takes US 97 east to the charmingly disheveled, semi-ghost town of **Shaniko** ★, population somewhere between 25 and 45. Shaniko was once an important wool-shipping center, but when the railroad bypassed the town in the early 1900s, its bloom soon faded. Today it comprises a few short blocks. Some of the buildings are pure ghost town, such as the tiny old jail, abandoned decades ago. Some are fixed up and tidy, such as the town's anchor, the **Shaniko Historic Hotel** *(541-489-3441 or 800-483-3441)*. The friendly owners don't mind if travelers mosey upstairs to look at the historic photographs in the halls.

From Shaniko, head south, then east on Oreg. 218, winding through virtually unpopulated juniper grasslands, where it seems that western meadowlarks sing their lilting melodies from every other fence post. Scan the grassy hillsides for pronghorn, antelopelike creatures that can run faster than any other mammal on the continent.

A few miles east of the John Day River, travelers come to the ❸ **Clarno Unit** of **John Day Fossil Beds National Monument** *(Visitor Center at Sheep Rock Unit. 541-987-2333)*. The badlands of the John Day River harbor one of the finest fossil beds in the world. Although most of what excites scientists remains hidden from the casual visitor, this mother lode can be glimpsed at the interpretive displays at the picnic area and on the nearby **Trail of the Fossils.** It stirs the imagination to gaze at a fossil leaf impression and realize it was made millions of years ago, when this portion of the Oregon high desert was a near subtropical rain forest.

The Cenozoic theme continues 20 miles up the highway in the town of—what else?—**Fossil** *(Town Hall, 401 Main St. 541-763-2698).* The town got its name in 1876 when a local rancher found fossilized bones on his spread. Today relics of the distant past still contribute to the identity of this town of 517. The porch of at least one house is lavishly decorated with fossils, and residents and visitors alike dig for fossils on an unmarked hillside behind the high school that is maintained for just that purpose *(more information available at Town Hall).* Even just using your hands, you easily can find soft rocks containing impressions of ancient leaves.

At the **Fossil Museum** *(1st and Washington Sts. 541-763-2698. Mid-May–mid-Oct., call for hours)* a large room is devoted to a fine exhibit entitled "Fossil Hunters of the High Desert." The other main room of the museum is a classic grab bag of local historic items, such as a sugar ration book from World War II, a 1918 grade school diploma, and a hank of hair labeled "hair." See if you can find the button from the Wheeler County Fair bearing a picture of a pig and a rose and the words "The Days of Swine and Roses."

Twenty miles north on Oreg. 19/218 lies a town much like Fossil but without the fossil mania. ❹ **Condon** barely interrupts the cattle ranches and wheat farms that characterize Gilliam County, population 1,900—that's for the whole county, not just the town. Check out David Peterson's one-chair barbershop *(2185 S. Main St.),*

Shaniko farm

where his price list once proclaimed that haircuts cost $8, or $200 for politicians. On the north end of town is the **Gilliam County Historical Society Depot Museum** *(Oreg. 19 at Burns Park. 541-384-4233. May-Oct. Wed.-Sun. and by appt.; donation),* which comprises a railroad depot, a barbershop, a pioneer log cabin, and a one-room schoolhouse, all filled with artifacts.

From Condon the drive curves northwest on Oreg. 206 through sagebrush-grassland hills punctuated with a few irrigated green patches near the John Day River. After about 60 miles the route returns to the Columbia River at its confluence with the Deschutes. Visitors may want to tarry at the oasis of the ❺ **Deschutes River State Recreation Area** *(541-739-2322),* which includes lush picnic grounds, historical signs, and hiking trails. A mile or two later the highway meets I-84, but before taking the interstate back to The Dalles, go under the overpass to **Celilo Park** *(541-296-1181),* where Celilo Falls was before disappearing beneath the reservoir of The Dalles Dam. The outdoor

Clarno Unit, John Day Fossil Beds National Monument

exhibit of historical photos shows the boiling rapids that for centuries were the Northwest's most famous salmon-fishing site and the region's trading crossroads.

The Wallowas

● 235 miles ● 2 to 3 days ● Late spring to early autumn ● Floods in winter 1996-97 damaged FR 39 portion of Hells Canyon National Scenic Byway; call ahead to check conditions (541-426-5546).

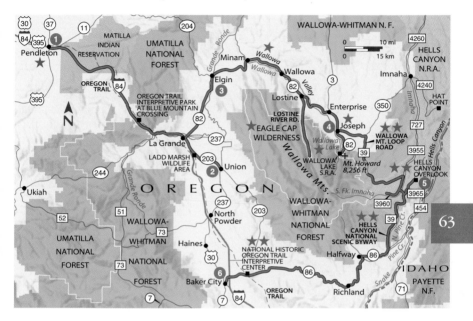

Okay, so the Wallowas (that's wuh-LAO-uhs) aren't a household name, like the Alps or the Rockies. But like those places, the Wallowas are more than a mountain range. They constitute a region, in this case a little-known area tucked away in northeast Oregon. The drive includes small towns where horses graze in backyards, sites rich in pioneer and Indian history, a bucolic valley sprinkled with tidy red barns, and a hotbed of artists that revolves around the sculpting of bronze. Along the way you will encounter much natural beauty, including old-growth ponderosa pine forests, wild-and-scenic rivers, many of the state's highest mountains, and the nation's deepest canyon.

Saddlemaker D.D. Potter in his Pendleton studio

At heart, ① **Pendleton**★ *(Chamber of Commerce 541-276-7411 or 800-547-8911)* is a cowboy town. Sure, it has pizza joints and satellite dishes, but Pendleton still serves as the commercial center for a vast ranching and farming region, and it still remembers its origins as a rip-snorting

64

Grainfield near Weston, northeast of Pendleton

frontier town where a man was more likely to wear spurs than a tie. Visit Pendleton's past at the **Umatilla County Historical Society Museum** *(108 S.W. Frazer Ave. 541-276-0012. Tues.-Sat.; adm. fee).*

In stylized form, Pendleton's cowboy character erupts every September in the form of the Pendleton Round-Up, one of the nation's largest rodeos and celebrations of things Western. The history of the roundup, which dates back to 1910, is depicted at the **Pendleton Round-Up/Happy Canyon Hall of Fame** *(Pendleton Round-Up Grounds, 1205 S.W. Court Ave. 541-278-0815. April-Oct. and by appt.; donation).*

The pastimes that defined the West as wild didn't all take place out on the range, as you'll learn as you explore Pendleton's spicy past with **Pendleton Underground Tours**★ *(37 S.W. Emigrant St. 541-276-0730. Call for hours and reservations; adm. fee).* The well-preserved network of underground rooms and tunnels leads to jail cells, a cardroom, saloons, a meat market, Chinese living quarters, an opium den, and, above ground, the site of a bordello—none still in operation, of course.

To many people, the name of this town is synonymous with the plaid wool shirts and patterned blankets manufactured at **Pendleton Woolen Mills** *(1307 S.E. Court Pl. 541-276-6911. Tours Mon.-Fri.).* Visitors can tour the 1909 mill—modernized inside—to see the legendary wool blankets being woven.

From Pendleton the route heads southeast on I-84, roughly paralleling the route of the Oregon Trail. After about 40 miles, travelers can plunge into the history of the trail by leaving the interstate at the Spring Creek exit and following the signs 3 miles to the **Oregon Trail Interpretive Park at Blue Mountain Crossing** *(La Grande Ranger District 541-963-7186. Mem. Day–Labor Day; fee).* This storied chapter of America's frontier saga is evoked by a trail with informational signs, people acting the parts of pioneers *(weekends),* and places where 150-year-old wagon-wheel ruts are still plainly visible.

A dozen miles southeast on I-84 brings motorists to **La Grande** *(La Grande/Union County Visitors & Convention Bureau 541-963-8588 or 800-848-9969)*, where the route turns northeast onto Oreg. 82. But first head southeast about 5 miles on Oreg. 203 to visit the 3,200-acre **Ladd Marsh Wildlife Area** *(Regional office, 107 20th St., La Grande. 541-963-2138. Map available)*. Here a nature trail, a bird-watching area, and other viewpoints provide fine looks at waterfowl (including some 16 species of ducks), raptors, and shorebirds, as well as elk, white-tailed and mule deer, and coyotes, among others. Then continue on Oreg. 203 about 8 miles to the historic town of ❷ **Union** and the **Union County Museum** *(333 S. Main St. 541-562-6003 or 800-848-9969. May-Oct. and by appt.; adm. fee)*. This museum of natural history, mining, period rooms, and pioneer exhibits was enhanced in 1996 with the acquisition of the collection "Cowboys Then & Now." It begins with Columbus's second voyage, when he brought cattle to Haiti, and continues to Hollywood Westerns and modern rodeos. Young cowpokes can don chaps and ten-gallon hats and climb aboard a saddle in the tack room display.

Back on Oreg. 82, mosey northward through cow country to ❸ **Elgin** and the **Elgin Opera House** *(104 N. 8th St. 541-437-3456. Call for hours and events)*. Completed in 1912, this colonial brick edifice was built to house the city offices, the city jail, the library, and a plush rococo theater. Only the theater remains, offering plays, movies, concerts, and tours of its interior, including a pinewood stage and an original backdrop signed and dated by actors in 1912.

From Elgin the road climbs east into the hills and along the Wallowa River through Minam Canyon. When the highway emerges from the canyon, just west of the town of Wallowa, motorists enter the heart of the region: **Wallowa Valley**★ *(Wallowa County Chamber of Commerce 541-426-4622 or 800-585-4121)*. Widely scattered ranches dot the countryside, their classic red barns vivid in the sunlight. Hills of grass and alfalfa ripple to a horizon of sawtooth peaks tipped with snow.

Mare and foal, near Wallowa

In the hamlet of Lostine, turn south on Lostine River Road. This paved and gravel byway winds 18 miles through farmland, forest, and a striking gorge before ending against the **Eagle Cap Wilderness**★ *(Visitor Center 541-426-5546)*. These 360,000 unspoiled acres encompass lush meadows, alpine lakes, broad glacial valleys, dense conifer forest, and wondrous high country. Most of 9,000-foot-plus peaks in Oregon stand in this wilderness area. Nearly 500 miles of trails invite travelers into the backcountry. Hearty, experienced backpackers can explore Eagle Cap on their own, and the less adventuresome can arrange guided treks—with your pack on the back of a llama or a horse. Depending on where you hike, backcountry visitors are likely to see elk, deer, hawks, and other wildlife. Lucky observers will spy mountain goats, peregrine falcons, bald eagles, and bighorn sheep.

Return to Oreg. 82 and continue southeast another 17 miles to **Enterprise** *(Wallowa County Chamber of Commerce 541-426-4622 or 800-585-4121)*. Here visitors can get their first look at the Wallowas' thriving bronze-casting industry at **Parks Bronze** *(331 Golf Course Rd. 541-426-4595. Tours Mon.-Fri.; adm. fee)*, which serves a number of prominent bronze sculptors as clients.

The region's artistic sensibility is also apparent 6 miles south in the small town of ❹ **Joseph**★ *(Wallowa County Chamber of Commerce 541-426-4622 or 800-585-4121)*. A few

blocks from the garages adorned with antlers are sidewalks lined with bronze sculptures, top-notch art galleries, and museums. Much of Joseph's surprising character stems from the presence of **Valley Bronze of Oregon**★ *(307 W. Alder St. 541-432-7551. Tours April-Oct. and by appt. Call for reservations; fee)*, the town's largest employer and one of the nation's leading bronze foundries. Tours reveal the alchemy of transforming this metal into the superb sculptures that grace the **Valley Bronze Showroom**★ *(18 S. Main St. 541-432-7445. Call for hours)*. Outstanding bronzes also occupy center stage a few blocks away at the **Manuel Museum** *(400 N. Main St. 541-432-7235. Closed Sat.-Sun. Dec.-April; adm. fee)*, home base for the famed sculptor David Manuel. But note this is called a museum, not a gallery; the handsome log building also contains a notable collection of Nez Perce artifacts. Through the museum, visitors can arrange for tours of **Joseph Bronze,** the small

Main Street, Joseph

Chief Joseph Memorial

foundry Manuel uses for much of his work.

The Nez Perce called the Wallowa Valley home until 1877, when Chief Joseph and his people were forced into their famous flight from the U.S. Army. Learn more of Nez Perce history by visiting the 1888 edifice housing the **Wallowa County Museum** *(110 S. Main St. 541-432-6095. Mem. Day–Sept.),* which also exhibits local pioneer artifacts.

Before proceeding east, take a mile-long excursion down Oreg. 82 to **Wallowa Lake★,** a classic glacial beauty cradled by moraines. Cruise along its eastern bank for 5 miles to the southern tip, which borders the Eagle Cap Wilderness. Then drop by pretty **Wallowa Lake State Recreation Area** *(541-432-4185. Mid-April–Oct.)* for a picnic or a stroll. For some elevated hiking, take the **Wallowa Lake Tramway★** *(541-432-5331. Mem. Day–Sept.; fare).* The thrillingly steep gondola ride at this former ski area hauls passengers 3,700 vertical feet up to the 8,256-foot summit of **Mount Howard.** Follow the 2.5 miles of trails to various lookout points and enjoy big-sky views of the valley, the wilderness, Snake River country, and various Idaho peaks.

From Joseph, go east 8 miles to Forest Road 39, turning right on the **Wallowa Mountain Loop Road★★,** part of the **Hells Canyon National Scenic Byway★★** *(Wallowa Mountains Visitor Center 541-426-5546).* The paved byway runs south through **Hells Canyon National Recreation Area,** up into mountainous terrain, some of it covered by old-growth ponderosa pine. These huge conifers with the ruddy, jigsaw-puzzle bark grow widely spaced, making cross-country hiking easy. Statuesque examples of ponderosa pine grow along the **Imnaha River,** which travelers can track by turning right onto Forest Road 3960, about 30 miles south of Joseph. Along this 10-mile spur lie a number of campgrounds, some only a few hundred yards from the river, including **Indian Crossing Campground.**

A few miles farther along Forest Road 39, turn off onto Forest Road 3965 and travel 3 miles to the ❺ **Hells Canyon Overlook★★.** Prepare to gawk. Despite Grand Canyon's fame, Hells Canyon is the deepest gorge in the

A Word from Chief Joseph

Chief Joseph, born in the Wallowa Valley in 1840, was tall, broad, and fair-minded. More diplomat than warrior, in 1877 he headed a group of Nez Perce who refused to leave land ceded to the U.S. through a fraudulent treaty. His attempts at peaceful negotiation were met with threats of forceful removal. The group's remarkable 15-week fighting retreat across Idaho and Montana ended in surrender near the Canadian border. Chief Joseph felt his peaceful tribe had been and continued to be treated unfairly, as he eloquently stated in 1879 in Washington, D.C.: "I have heard talk and talk, but nothing is done.... It makes my heart sick when I remember all the good words and all the broken promises. I know that my race must change. We only ask an even chance to live as other men live.... The earth is the mother of all people, and all people should have equal rights upon it."

67

United States; its depth to the river of 8,043 feet beats out its Arizona cousin by some 2,000 feet. From the overlook observers can gaze down at the erosive handiwork of the Snake River or far east at the Seven Devils Mountains in Idaho. Especially striking are sunrise and sunset, when the furrows of the side canyons create a stark world of sun and shadow.

As motorists follow Forest Road 39 south along pretty North Pine Creek, the ponderosa pines are gradually replaced by deciduous trees and the mountains melt into hills. Where North Pine Creek empties into Pine Creek, the drive turns west on Oreg. 86, curving through beautiful hill

Hells Canyon and the Snake River

country. To the south, grass and sagebrush roll to the distant horizon. To the north, conifer forest rises from the grasslands and slopes up to the peaks of the Wallowa Mountains. Isolated ranches occupy green valleys laced with creeks, the kind of spreads cowboys must have envisioned when they spoke wistfully of "settling down someday."

After about an hour's drive on Oreg. 86, you can almost hear echoes of the pioneer past emanating from this frontier landscape. That's perfect, because it sets the mood for the **National Historic Oregon Trail Interpretive Center**★★ *(Oreg. 86, 5 miles E of Baker City. 541-523-1843. Adm. fee).* Atop Flagstaff Hill, near some well-preserved traces of the Oregon Trail, the Interpretive Center gives a visceral sense of the trail experience. Photos of a pioneer family resting by their wagon, an interactive display in

Hells Canyon National Recreation Area

which children (and adults) make hard choices about
what provisions they would take, a living history presentation in which an actress plays the meticulously
researched role of a pioneer on the trail, and more. It all
adds up to a complex portrait of the triumphs and tribula-
tions of the 2,000-mile trek from Missouri to Oregon.

The drive ends in ❻ **Baker City** *(Baker County Visitor &
Convention Bureau 541-523-3356 or 800-523-1235),* but the
history continues. More than a hundred houses and commercial buildings from the old days lend a venerable air
to Baker City's extensive historic district. Visitors can catch
gold fever at the **U.S. Bank** *(2000 Main St. 541-523-7791.
Mon.-Fri.),* where a gold collection dating back more than
80 years is on display. The centerpiece is the pear-size
Armstrong nugget. The cavernous **Oregon Trail Regional
Museum** *(2480 Grove St. 541-523-9308. Mid-April–Oct.; donation)* brims with the expected pioneer artifacts and with
several unexpected exhibits, notably a fine collection of
rocks, minerals, fossils, and semiprecious stones.

Walla Walla Wander

● **175 miles** ● **2 days** ● **Spring through autumn**

Whitman Mission National Historic Site

This little corner of southeast Washington offers quiet, pastoral pleasures. Oh, there's a top-notch science museum, some notable historic sites, and the immense presence of the Columbia River, but most of the route is less flashy. Travelers begin in history-rich Walla Walla, proceed west to some pocket wineries, and then follow the Columbia River up to the Tri-Cities for some urban pursuits. From there the route passes through wheat-furred hills and towns with grain elevators for skyscrapers to conclude at a dramatic canyon waterfall.

Visitors have been known to stroll the comfortable old downtown of ❶ **Walla Walla** (*Chamber of Commerce, 29 E. Sumach St. 509-525-0850. Walking tour brochure available*) saying the town's name over and over, it's just so satisfying. As documented by Meriwether Lewis and William Clark, the Native American meaning of the name is "many waters" or "running water." The town teems with history—Main Street was built on a Nez Perce trail leading to the Columbia River. Notable structures include the **Kirkman House** *(214 N. Colville St. 509-529-4373. Call for appt.; donation)*, an impressive 1880 Italianate open for tours. Just beyond downtown sprawls the major historic complex of the **Fort Walla Walla Museum**★ *(755 Myra Rd. 509-525-7700. Tues.-Sun. April-Oct.; adm. fee)*. Five warehouse-size buildings exhibit all sorts of pioneer artifacts, including a 33-mule team harnessed to a huge combine. An 1880 railway station and an 1859 cabin are among the 16 original and reconstructed structures scattered around the grounds.

Just ten minutes west from Walla Walla on US 12 lies one of the key sites in the history of the Oregon Territory (which included present-day Washington): the **Whitman Mission National Historic Site** *(509-529-2761. Adm. fee)*. Little remains of this important Oregon Trail haven, but the fine small museum and interpretive paths tell the story of Marcus Whitman and the missionaries who settled this site in the 1830s. Long-simmering tensions prompted the local Cayuse in 1847 to kill Whitman and 12 other whites before releasing the remaining hostages from the mission, starting a war that figured importantly in the decision to make Oregon a United States territory.

Eric Dunham, assistant winemaker, L'Ecole No. 41

71

About 5 miles west of the mission the route breezes through the rather small agricultural hamlet of **Lowden,** where cast-off farming equipment serves as lawn ornaments. But Lowden also holds two estimable if small wineries, right on the highway. Many aficionados consider **Woodward Canyon Winery** *(509-525-4129)* one of the state's finest. **L'Ecole No. 41** *(509-525-0940. Tours by appt.)*, as the name implies, is housed in a 1915 grade school. Chalkboards and kid-size drinking fountains still exist amid the tanks and oak barrels.

Continue west until a broad expanse of the **Columbia River** blocks the way, at which point US 12 wisely swings north and follows the river up to the **Tri-Cities** *(Visitor & Convention Bureau 509-735-8486 or 800-254-5824)*. Pasco, Kennewick, and Richland have grown together into a contiguous urban area that is home to more than 175,000 people. Yet this remains farming country, as evidenced by farmers' markets, wineries, and fields that border highways and subdivisions.

As you enter the Tri-Cities from the south, pause at ❷ **Sacajawea State Park** *(509-545-2361. Call for hours)*. For centuries travelers have stopped at this point—the most important river confluence in the western U.S., where the Columbia and Snake Rivers collide (although dams have tamed that collision). Lewis and Clark camped here in 1805; their journey is detailed at the park's Interpretive Center. A few miles farther into **Pasco,** travelers can learn much more about Lewis and Clark and the area's history at the **Franklin County Historical Museum** *(305 N. 4th Ave. 509-547-3714. Tues.-Sat.),* housed in a 1911 Carnegie

72

library building. The county's two pillars—agriculture and the railroads—get especially thorough treatment. Check out the Northern Pacific ads luring people West to "Pasco, Queen City of the Plains."

The history lessons continue just across the Columbia in **Kennewick** at the **East Benton County Museum** *(205 Keewaydin Dr. 509-582-7704. Tues.-Sat.; donation).* Amid exhibits on early farming is a highly regarded collection of more than 2,800 Columbia River Indian gem points (arrowheads, spearheads, and more), made of agate, petrified wood, and jasper.

Displays of a different sort await in ❸ **Richland** at the **Columbia River Exhibition of History, Science, and Technology**★ *(95 Lee Blvd. 509-943-9000. Adm. fee),* which opened in early 1997, incorporating the former Hanford Science Center. Note that just northwest of the Tri-Cities lies the 560 square miles of the Hanford Site, once the coun-

Palouse Falls State Park

try's largest producer of nuclear materials for the military, now the largest storehouse of radioactive waste in the U.S. This new museum deals extensively with both the production of nuclear weapons and the technology involved in cleaning up the contamination. Exhibits also cover robotics, hydropower, and laser technology, as well as the human history and geology of the area.

The nine Hanford reactors (now shut down) were built along the Columbia, whose cold waters cooled the reactors' thermonuclear cores. The nation's passion for security was one reason the site's 50-mile stretch of river, known as the Hanford Reach, was kept off limits from 1943 until the mid-1970s; as a result it's the only section of the Columbia between Bonneville Dam and the Canadian border that hasn't been dammed into a reservoir. Travelers can visit this free-flowing reminder of the Columbia's glory days aboard a 26-person boat operated by **Columbia River Journeys**★ *(509-943-0231. May-Oct.; fare).* The four-hour trip takes passengers 38 miles upriver, past sand dunes, massive white cliffs, and miles of the sagebrush-grasslands that typify this arid country. The captain may pull in for good looks at an osprey nest and a black-crowned night heron nesting colony—great blue herons, terns, cormorants, great egrets, huge white pelicans laboriously flapping their 9-foot wingspans, all frequent the reach. While the boat cruises past some of the silenced reactors, the captain tells of the some 50,000 workers who labored here during the peak war years and made the plutonium for the bomb dropped on Nagasaki, Japan, in 1945.

Just south of Pasco the drive cuts east on Wash. 124 across the rolling sagebrush-steppe, almost all of which now grows dry-land wheat or, with the help of irrigation, fruits and vegetables. Five miles along turn north to visit **Ice Harbor Dam** *(U.S. Army Corps of Engineers 509-547-7781)* on the Snake River, where you can see the dam and power plant, and view exhibits and count fish at the Visitor Center *(April-Oct.)*. After that it's a 40-mile run through the fields to the intersection with US 12.

Before returning to Walla Walla, drive northeast to the agricultural town of ❹ **Dayton** *(Chamber of Commerce 509-382-4825)*. Its cozy downtown and noteworthy historical district include the elaborate, Italianate 1887 **Columbia County Courthouse** *(Main and 3rd Sts. Mon.-Fri.)*, Washington's oldest. A block away is the state's oldest railroad depot, the 1881 **Dayton Historical Depot,** now a museum *(Commercial Ave. and 2nd St. 509-382-2026. Tues.-Sat.; adm. fee. Walking tour map available)*. Venture into the elegant Victorian **Weinhard Hotel** *(235 E. Main St. 509-382-4032)*, or head next door to the **Wenaha Gallery** *(219 E. Main St. 509-382-2124. Tues.-Sat.)*, where top local and national artists display their works.

To end the drive in dramatic fashion, continue on US 12 to Wash. 261 and turn northwest. This backroad leads to **Little Goose Dam** and **Lyons Ferry State Park** *(509-646-3252. Late March–late Oct.)*, but the final attraction remains ❺ **Palouse Falls State Park** *(Campground open late March–Sept.)*. The Palouse River takes a showy, 198-foot dive into the enormous basalt basin it has carved out and then flows on down a starkly beautiful stone-wall canyon. A precarious trail edges along the cliff wall and a safer, maintained trail leads along the rim above the falls.

Whither Hanford?

While the Hanford Site is one of the country's most contaminated nuclear locations, a 530-square-mile buffer zone surrounds the production area, comprised of virtually pristine sagebrush—the last large remnant of this rare habitat in the U.S., perhaps in the world. In the name of security, Hanford was built in an isolated, barely developed area. Helicopters, guard dogs, and armed sentries kept people away, inadvertently preserving the land. Now that the Cold War is over and Hanford's nuclear mission has ended, the U.S. Fish & Wildlife Service, county governments, local farmers, environmentalists, and other suitors are lined up at the gates. Some want to protect the natural environment, some want to develop the land, and some want to do a bit of both.

Spokane Loop

● 250 miles ● 2 to 3 days ● Spring through autumn

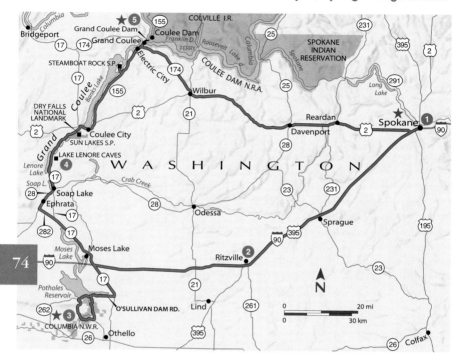

Crossing the Cascade Range from western to eastern Washington is almost like crossing a national boundary. Forests, mountains, seashores, big cities, and legendary rainfall give way to grasslands, canyons, farms, and a high desert climate. Spokane, where this route begins, is something of an anomaly, as it's a big city and it lies in a wetter zone graced by pine forest. But when this loop drive heads southwest, it soon descends into flat wheat fields and small towns before entering the channeled scablands: shrub steppe gouged in the geologic past by cataclysmic floods. The route follows the lakes of the biggest gouge—the Grand Coulee—north to the colossal dam of the same name and then back east to Spokane.

❶ **Spokane** ★ *(Visitor Center 509-747-3230 or 800-248-3230)* is one of those happy municipalities with a thriving downtown that is central to its past, present, and future. Many historic buildings line the banks of the Spokane River, such as the old **Flour Mill** *(624 W. Mallon Ave.),* now full of shops, and the **Davenport Hotel** *(807 W. Sprague Ave. 509-455-8888),* which is undergoing an extensive facelift. Mixed in with the old are modern neighbors, such as the

Spokane Opera House *(334 W. Spokane Falls Blvd. 509-353-6500)*. The downtown got a big boost from the 1974 World's Fair, whose site is preserved as **Riverfront Park★★** *(509-625-6600),* populated by street musicians, joggers, parents pushing strollers, craftspeople hawking their wares, cyclists, and people fishing from bridges. Its 100-plus acres hold an **Art Walk** comprising numerous sculptures, the **Spokane IMAX Theater** *(509-625-6604. Adm. fee),* two historic hydroelectric power plants, an amusement park, and the exquisitely carved 1907 **Antique Looff Carrousel** *(Closed early Jan.– mid-March; fee).* The park also encompasses **Spokane Falls,** a flamboyant series of cascades that can be admired from numerous viewpoints on the river's banks and from a **gondola** *(April-Sept.; fee)* that crosses above. Note: During midsummer the falls virtually dry up as the regional utility diverts the water to its hydroelectric facility.

Reflection on Spokane Opera House, Riverfront Park

Among the city's many other parks is **Manito Park and Gardens★** *(4 W. 21st Ave. 509-625-6622),* set amid some charming historic neighborhoods. This large park blends ponderosa pine forest; recreational areas; and gardens, including Rose Hill, the serene Japanese Garden, the Gaiser Conservatory, and Duncan Garden, a lavish formal garden that peaks from mid-July through September.

During the late 1800s and early 1900s, many wealthy residents built showy mansions in the neighborhood called **Browne's Addition,** just west of downtown. Stop by **Patsy Clark's** *(W. 2208 2nd Ave. 509-838-8300),* a 26-room, 9-fireplace palace commissioned in 1895 that currently houses a swanky restaurant. A major regional museum awaits 3 blocks away at the **Cheney Cowles Museum and Historic Campbell House★** *(2316 W. 1st Ave. 509-456-3931 ext. 101 or 122. Closed Mon.; adm. fee).* Here, thematic exhibits describe the development of the Inland Northwest and Plateau Indian cultures. Built in 1898 during Spokane's so-called age of elegance, the Campbell House has been beautifully restored and furnished in period style.

Heading southwest from Spokane on I-90/US 395, you'll soon hit wheat country. In summer there seems to be nothing for miles but blue sky and golden fields. After an hour you'll come to the typical eastern Washington town of

Wheat crop ready for harvest, near Ritzville

2 Ritzville *(City Clerk 509-659-1930).* Here, on Saturdays, the clack of pool balls and country-western music echo off the 19th-century brick buildings; the theater (the Ritz, of course) shows movies only on weekends; and the grain elevators and railroad tracks are right downtown.

Head west on I-90 toward **Moses Lake,** and then drive south on Wash. 17 and O'Sullivan Dam Road to the **3 Columbia National Wildlife Refuge★** *(509-488-2668).* The best time to visit is from March through September. The refuge encompasses a large section of the **Drumheller Channels National Landmark.** Apocalyptic ice age floods ravaged this high-desert landscape, creating canyons, stony ridges, lakes, ponds, and uncovering spectacular basalt column formations. An extensive network of roads and hiking trails allow visitors to search this starkly beautiful landscape for hawks, pelicans, herons, beavers, coyotes, and other wildlife.

Enjoying Soap Lake

Back in Moses Lake, head northwest on Wash. 17, then branch off on Wash. 282 to Ephrata and the **Grant County Historical Museum★** *(742 Basin St. N.W. 509-754-3334. Closed Wed. early May–Sept.; adm. fee).* Dozens of historic structures packed with artifacts help this large history museum to powerfully evoke the everyday life of 19th- and early 20th-century eastern Washington.

One fun exhibit challenges visitors to identify a selection of unlabeled pioneer artifacts: Answers include a huckleberry picker, a hay knife, a cornhusker…the rest you'll have to figure out for yourself.

Take Wash. 28 back to Wash. 17 and continue north, skirting the eastern shore of **Soap Lake,** so called due to the natural chemicals that give it a soapy feel. At **Lenore Lake,** hike up to the ❹ **Lake Lenore Caves** *(Take gravel road off Wash. 17).* Another 10 miles brings you to the overlook and Visitor Center *(June-Sept.)* at **Dry Falls National Landmark** *(Sun Lakes State Park 509-632-5583).* Be glad you weren't here during the ice ages, when a series of monster floods clawed the basalt, leaving behind deep rips in the earth, such as the 400-foot-deep, 3.5-mile-wide canyon below the viewpoint. At its head are the rock cliffs over which the flood waters poured when Dry Falls was wet, creating a cascade that would dwarf Niagara Falls. Today, the park offers swimming, fishing, hiking, and boating. A steep but short trail leads down to the canyon.

Just beyond Dry Falls, the route turns east onto US 2 then strikes north on Wash. 155 along the shore of **Banks Lake.** Near its north end lies **Steamboat Rock State Park** *(509-633-1304),* where you can fish, swim, picnic, or hike up the 700-foot-high butte to its flat top for some big views.

Another monolith rises 13 miles north, only this one was made by the U.S. Bureau of Reclamation, not nature. "Big" is the operative word at ❺ **Grand Coulee Dam ★** *(Visitor Center, Wash. 155. 509-633-9265).* At the Visitor Center or while taking a guided tour, you'll be showered with evidence of the dam's size. At 550 feet high and almost a mile across, it's one of the largest concrete structures in the world, containing enough concrete to build a 4-foot-wide sidewalk twice around the equator. Other fun facts: Workers use bikes to get around inside the dam, its spillway is about the same size as Niagara Falls, and some of the bolts in the dam weigh 960 pounds. To grasp the immensity of the dam in a literally visceral way, drive along its top, stop in the middle, and peek over the edge at the dizzying slope of the spillway as it plunges down to the river.

When your pulse returns to normal, you may want to enjoy the moving views from the incline elevator, or make plans to take in the flashy laser show *(Mem. Day–Sept.)* that uses the dam as a screen each summer night. From the dam it's a 90-mile drive through wheat country via Wash. 174 and US 2 back to Spokane.

Ice Age Floods

Near the end of the last ice age, about 17,000 years ago, a finger of the continental ice sheet poked south into what is now Idaho and dammed the Clark Fork. Water backed up for many years, forming gigantic Lake Missoula, which covered thousands of square miles. When the ice dam finally gave way, water raged out of Clark Fork Canyon. Tearing west at interstate highway speeds through the larger canyons, this flood scoured off hundreds of feet of soil and gouged out deep canyons, which are especially evident in eastern Washington. This process is believed to have occurred again and again in the last ice age and repeatedly in earlier ice ages—up to a hundred times all told.

Heart of the Cascades★

● 380 miles ● 3 to 4 days ● Late spring through autumn ● Crosses some moderately high passes where snow can close roads from late autumn to early spring.

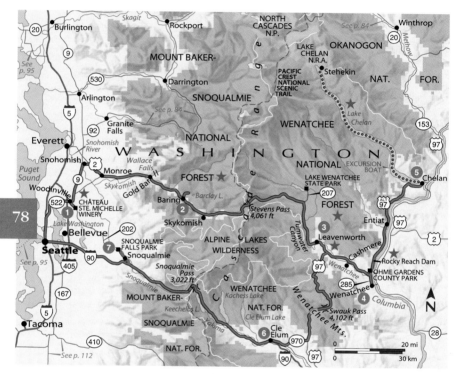

A major city, small towns, bucolic byways, grand wilderness, coastline, apple country, lush west-side forests and dry east-side forests: This drive is like a Washington sampler. It climbs over the Cascades, giving travelers access to waterfalls, forests, rivers, mountains, and a handful of old logging and mining towns. On the east side the loop route descends to a mock-Bavarian village, a historic little town, and the apple capital of the state. A spur leads north along the Columbia River to the departure point for a cruise deep into the wilds. As it circles back to Seattle, the drive again crosses a prime expanse of the Cascades.

This drive starts in Seattle (see Washington's Waterfront drive, p. 95) and goes northeast up Wash. 522. At **Woodinville,** head south 1 mile on Wash. 202 to ❶ **Château Ste. Michelle Winery**★ *(14111 N.E. 145th St. 206-488-3300)*. Behind the elaborate, French-château facade lies one of the state's largest and most acclaimed wineries,

Château Ste. Michelle Winery, Woodinville

open for tours. Walk the 87-acre sprawl of formal gardens and experimental vineyards while arguing the merits of your favorite vintages.

Two miles past Woodinville on Wash. 522, go north on Wash. 9 to the old timber and dairy town of **Snohomish** *(Chamber of Commerce 360-568-2526)*. Need an ornate Victorian fish bowl stand? You've come to the right place. In addition to numerous antique stores, hundreds of dealers cluster in labyrinthine emporiums that feel like huge attics that haven't been cleaned out in decades. Many of the buildings are themselves antiques; check out the old **Oxford Saloon** *(913 1st St.)* and the historic houses just north of downtown.

Go east on US 2, which soon joins the Skykomish River and heads up into the Cascades. For 60 or 70 miles travelers meander first through the **Mount Baker-Snoqualmie National Forest**★ *(Skykomish Ranger District 360-677-2414)* and then the **Wenatchee National Forest**★ *(Lake Wenatchee Ranger District 509-763-3103)*. Dozens of trails invite you to park your car and hike into the high country. Even before the highway enters the national forests, just outside the little town of **Gold Bar,** a fine trail of moderate difficulty leads to 265-foot **Wallace Falls.** A 2.2-mile path starts a few miles north of ❷ **Baring,** leading along Barclay Creek to Barclay Lake. It's virtually flat, pretty, and, therefore, crowded at prime times. Farther east, consider a short side trip on Wash. 207 to **Lake Wenatchee State Park** *(509-763-3101)*, where hiking

Crossing sign, Skykomish

Visitors to Leavenworth

Transpacific Flight

80

In 1931 Washington native Clyde Pangborn and Hugh Herndon, Jr., landed their single-engine plane in Wenatchee, Washington, completing the first nonstop flight across the Pacific. The 41-hour, 4,500-mile journey almost didn't get off the ground, however. First, the flyers were charged with espionage and detained nearly two months in Japan. Then their little Bellanca, designed to carry 5,600 pounds, weighed in at 9,000, due to the enormous load of fuel. The Tokyo airport's runway, impossibly short, necessitated takeoff from a remote beach on Honshū island. The pilots jettisoned their landing gear to save more weight, making it a rough but nonlethal belly landing.

is augmented by canoeing, boating, fishing, horseback riding, and other activities.

From the Wash. 207 junction, US 2 descends alongside the **Wenatchee River** as it plunges through dramatic **Tumwater Canyon.** At the canyon's end, encircled by mountains, lies the town of ❸ **Leavenworth** ★ *(Chamber of Commerce 509-548-5807).* Reminiscent of the Alps, you say? That's what the good people of Leavenworth thought, too, when they decided in the 1960s to transform their moribund timber town into a mock-Bavarian Alps village in order to attract tourists. Virtually the entire main part of town went Bavarian with a vengeance. The hotels and restaurants look Bavarian, right down to the hundreds of window boxes bright with flowers and the carved wooden rails of the many balconies. Even the Mexican restaurant and *Die Wascherei* (the laundromat) located blocks off the main drag maintain the theme. Add a town square, an oompah band, reasonably authentic German food and beer, and the effect is pleasing, though undeniably hokey.

Leavenworth is also a jumping-off point for hiking, rafting, skiing, canoeing, fishing, and other outdoor pursuits. Travelers can start right in town at **Waterfront Park** along the Wenatchee River and on adjacent **Blackbird Island.** Interpretive signs dot several of the trails, informing hikers about the Indian village that used to occupy this site and about the way the wetlands absorb floodwaters.

A short drive through a drier, east-side landscape replete with mostly apple and pear orchards leads to **Cashmere** *(Chamber of Commerce 509-782-1511).* In season, stop at **Bob's Apple Barrel** on US 2, for fresh fruit, cider, or fruit milkshakes. Or tour the **Aplets & Cotlets Candy Factory** *(117 Mission Ave. 509-782-2191. Tours daily except Sat.-Sun. Jan.-March),* which daily produces more than 15,000 pounds of regionally famous fruit candy. The sweet smells in this factory will almost knock off the silly hats that tour participants must wear to meet health codes.

Nearby in place but distant in time is the **Chelan County Historical Society's Museum and Pioneer Village** ★ *(600 Cottage Ave. 509-782-3230. March-Oct.; adm. fee).* The recently expanded museum building displays regional wildlife, mostly birds; minerals and petrified wood whose colors and patterns resemble fine sculptures; and a remarkable collection of thousands of prehistoric and more recent Indian artifacts. Outside, browse through the 20 or so

19th-century buildings filled with pioneer artifacts, including a jail, a mission, a saloon, and a school.

The fruit trees, particularly the apple orchards, multiply as US 2 continues toward **④ Wenatchee** *(Chamber of Commerce 509-662-2116 or 800-57-APPLE).* Here the apple is king, as evident at the **Washington Apple Commission Visitor Center** *(2900 Euclid Ave. 509-663-9600. Closed Sat.-Sun. Jan.-April),* which is part store, part interpretive center, and part propaganda. Stop and find out which apples are best for baking, why coating apples with ice stops them from freezing, and how Washington produces 80 to 90 million boxes of apples a year, more than half of all the apples grown in the U.S. Visitors also can buy apple clocks, apple paperweights, apple checker sets, and more.

Apples also enjoy lofty status at the **North Central Washington Museum**★ *(127 S. Mission St. 509-664-3340. Closed weekends in Jan.; adm. fee),* where an entire exhibit hall is devoted to the industry. Check out the 1920s packing line and the artistic labels for various old companies, such as "Teacher's Pet" and "Yum-yum" apples. The museum also features an exhibit on the Clovis people, who inhabited the area some 10,000 years ago, and displays on Washington native Clyde Pangborn, who with Hugh Herndon, Jr., made the first nonstop transpacific flight in 1931, going 4,500 miles from Japan to Wenatchee (see sidebar p. 80).

Need a respite from the road? High on a bluff above the Columbia River near the north end of town you'll find

Apple orchards, near Cashmere

sanctuary at **Ohme Gardens County Park** *(3327 Ohme Rd. 509-662-5785. Mid-April–mid-Oct.; adm. fee)*, a green place of native trees and low-growing plants on 9 sloping acres. It's manicured, but discreetly, so that it is more wild high country than formal garden, with overlooks that take in the Columbia, the Wenatchee Valley, and the Cascades.

When your soul is sufficiently serene, drive north on US 97A along the west bank of the Columbia to **Rocky Reach Dam** ★ *(509-663-8121. Mid-Feb.–Dec.)*. During the summer, travelers can watch salmon head upriver and take guided generator tours—pretty standard dam stuff. But Rocky Reach harbors surprises. As in an anthill, galleries have been carved out deep inside the power-house. Two are amazingly extensive, each running for hundreds of yards overlooking the thrumming row of turbines. The Gallery of the Columbia covers in vast detail the prehistory and history of the area, from geological formation to ancient peoples to early European explorers to the steamboats that plied the Columbia. In even greater detail, the Gallery of Electricity provides a chronology of this energy source, from lodestones to Ben Franklin to Thomas Edison to radio telescopes.

82

Lady of the Lake passenger ferry from Chelan to Stehekin

Continue north on US 97A about 30 miles to **Lake Chelan** ★ *(Chelan Ranger District 509-682-2576)*. This fjord-like glacial lake thrusts 55 miles northwest, far into the wilderness, all the way into the southern part of Lake Chelan National Recreation Area. The portion of the lake close to **5 Chelan** *(Chamber of Commerce 509-682-2022)* and the highway is a motel- and condo-lined playground, popular among boaters, fishermen, water-skiers, and sailors. The upper part, accessible only by boat or small plane, is a wild place of dense forest and looming mountains. Two excursion boats *(Lake Chelan Boat Co. 509-682-4584)* travel the length of the lake to the tiny hamlet of **Stehekin.** Many go along just for the ride, which includes narration and a short stay in Stehekin. Or spend the night in the village and savor the surroundings and explore the many trails that fan out along the lake and into the mountains.

Retrace your route all the way back to the intersection of US 97 and US 2 just west of Cashmere and continue south on US 97. Proceed 35 miles through the Wenatchee National Forest to Wash. 970, then head west past ❻ **Cle Elum,** on I-90. Take the interstate back toward Seattle,

Farmland along Wash. 97, near Swauk Pass

once again crossing a striking expanse of the Cascades. And, once again, hiking trails abound. Many start at **Snoqualmie Pass** and vicinity, forging north amid the old-growth forest, snowy peaks, tundra, and creeks of the **Alpine Lakes Wilderness.** But this area, a mere hour on the interstate from Seattle, gets crowded, especially during summer and on weekends. Rangers at the **Snoqualmie Pass Visitor Information Center** *(206-434-6111. Thurs.-Sun. Or call North Bend Ranger District 206-888-1421. Mon.-Fri.)* suggest trying the trails south of I-90, such as the **Annette Lake Trail** and the **Asahel Curtis Nature Trail.**

Half an hour west of the pass the Snoqualmie River takes a showy, 268-foot dive over **Snoqualmie Falls,** a few miles north of **Snoqualmie** *(Chamber of Commerce 206-888-4440).* At ❼ **Snoqualmie Falls Park,** a trail along the rim of the river gorge, and an overlook provide several vantage points from which to contemplate this plunge. The dining room at luxurious **Salish Lodge** *(206-888-2556 or 800-826-6124),* adjacent to the park, also commands a front-row seat of the river's theatrics. After a good meal and a good long look, return to I-90 and Seattle.

North Cascades ★

● **340 miles** ● **3 to 4 days** ● **Late spring to early autumn** ● **Snow typically closes the road from Ross Dam through Washington Pass from November to April. There are no major services on Wash. 20 for the 86 miles between Marblemount and Winthrop.**

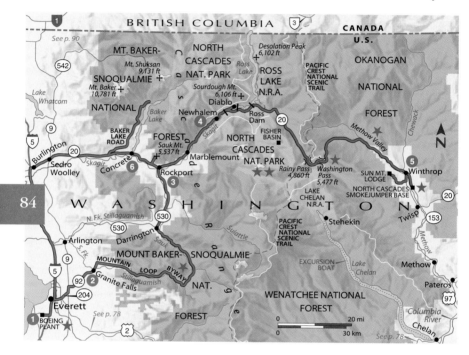

See p. 90

BRITISH COLUMBIA

CANADA
U.S.

MT. BAKER-
Mt. Shuksan
9,131 ft
SNOQUALMIE
Mt. Baker
10,781 ft

NORTH CASCADES NAT. PARK

Desolation Peak
6,102 ft

PACIFIC CREST NATIONAL SCENIC TRAIL

OKANOGAN

ROSS LAKE N.R.A.

NATIONAL

Lake Whatcom

NATIONAL

Sourdough Mt.
6,106 ft
Diablo
Newhalem

Baker Lake

FOREST

FOREST

Ross Dam

Methow Valley

Chewack

Burlington
Sedro Woolley
Concrete

BAKER LAKE ROAD

Sauk Mt.
5,537 ft
Marblemount
Rockport

FOREST

NORTH CASCADES NAT. PARK

FISHER BASIN

Rainy Pass
4,860 ft

Washington Pass
5,477 ft

SUN MT. LODGE

NORTH CASCADES SMOKEJUMPER BASE

Winthrop

N

LAKE CHELAN N.R.A.

N. Fk. Stillaguamish

Arlington
Darrington

MOUNT BAKER-SNOQUALMIE

Suiattle

PACIFIC CREST NATIONAL SCENIC TRAIL

Stehekin

Twisp

MOUNTAIN LOOP
BYWAY
Granite Falls
Everett

NAT.

EXCURSION BOAT

Lake Chelan

Methow

Pateros

WENATCHEE NATIONAL FOREST

FOREST

Boeing Plant

0   20 mi
0   30 km

Columbia River
Chelan

See p. 78

84

Washington may be home to excessively civilized coffee, and it may be headquarters of computer wizardry, but the state also harbors places where wolves howl and humans seldom tread. This route shows off Washington's wild side. Starting from Everett, the drive follows a scenic backroad through Mount Baker-Snoqualmie National Forest. It then joins the lone highway that cuts across the North Cascades, one of the wildest places in America. After an incongruous stop in a Wild West theme town, climb back over the Cascades and trace the Skagit River before returning to civilization, where you can discuss black bear sightings over lattes.

Boeing Plant, Everett

The journey begins with a bang, many bangs, actually, on a tour of the noisy but interesting ❶ **Boeing Plant** ★ (*Wash. 526. 206-342-4801. Tours Mon.-Fri.*) in **Everett.** Watch

747s being assembled in a huge building said to be the world's largest space under one roof (472 million cubic feet). Historic buildings of various styles decorate Everett's downtown, and the mansions of turn-of-the-century timber barons still line Grand and Rucker Avenues on the town's north end.

From Everett, work your way over to Wash. 92 via US 2, Wash. 204, and Wash. 9, and head east. Beyond ❷ **Granite Falls** continue east on the **Mountain Loop Byway★**, which cuts deep into the **Mount Baker-Snoqualmie National Forest** *(Darrington Ranger District 206-259-7911)*. The 55-mile byway, of which 14 miles are unpaved, follows the tumbling South Fork Stillaguamish and Sauk Rivers and borders three wilderness areas. Dozens of trails vein out from the byway, inviting hikers of all levels into the woods. Hardy types may want to labor 3 miles up to the top of **Mount Pilchuck** for a view of Puget Sound, the San Juan Islands, and a vast expanse of the Cascades. Those looking for more of a stroll would enjoy the **Big Four Ice Caves Trail,** which starts with a boardwalk through a marsh and winds about a mile through fine forest to an ice cave at the base of some dramatic cliffs. But admire the ice formations (which usually start taking shape in August) from afar; literally tons of ice occasionally fall from the ceiling. The 3-mile **Old Sauk Trail** provides another easy walk, slipping through lush old-growth forest along the southwest bank of the Sauk River; look for ospreys, waterfowl, and, in late summer and fall, spawning salmon.

Wildflowers along Sauk Mountain Trail, near Rockport

At the end of the byway, in Darrington, scoot up Wash. 530 to ❸ **Rockport.** Drive west on Wash. 20 to **Rockport State Park** *(360-853-8461. April-Nov.)* and head up the **Sauk Mountain Trail,** which leads through a stand of old-growth Douglas-fir to generous vistas of the Cascades. The 20-mile stretch of the **Skagit River** between Concrete and Marblemount is renowned as a haven for bald eagles. Between December and February, with numbers usually peaking in January, as many as 500 eagles come here to feed on migrating salmon *(Upper Skagit Eagles Festival 360-853-7009)*. Early in the morning, when the eagles are most active, you're likely to see America's avian symbol gather along the river to feed on carcasses of spawned-out salmon. Several operators run float trips for eagle-watchers.

As you proceed east on Wash. 20, the Skagit River Valley begins narrowing and the land begins rising. Six miles past Marblemount the route crosses into the **Ross Lake National Recreation Area,** part of **North Cascades National Park**★★ *(Headquarters 360-856-5700).* The park is one of the wildest places in the lower 48. Very few roads and little development have touched these half million acres of sawtooth peaks, waterfalls, abundant wildlife, glaciers, meadows, icy creeks, and lakes. You'll get a breathtaking look from Wash. 20, but such a wilderness should be seen on foot. Many trails start from the highway; stop for hiking information near ❹ **Newhalem** at the **North Cascades Visitor Center** *(Wash. 20. 206-386-4495. Daily mid-April–mid-Nov., weekends rest of year).* While you're there, walk the boardwalk to view the Picket Range and see the informative interpretive displays and videos.

A mile away lies Newhalem proper. Seattle City Light built this tidy little company town for the workers who operate the three dams you'll see a few miles farther up the road. Several short, easy trails fan out from town,

Canoeists on Ross Lake

including the **Trail of the Cedars,** a 0.3-mile interpretive loop amid overwhelming cedar trees.

Six miles up Wash. 20 a short side road leads to **Diablo,** jumping-off point for **Seattle City Light Tours** *(206-684-3030. Mid-June–Aug. Thurs.-Mon., Sept. Sat.-Sun.; adm. fee).* The full four-hour tour includes a slide show, a ride up **Sourdough Mountain** on a historic incline railway, a boat ride across **Diablo Lake,** and dinner. Travelers also can gaze upon this blue-green lake from a highway overlook; glacial sediments, also known as rock flour, account for the startling color. A few miles up the road another overlook provides views of another blue-green beauty, **Ross Lake,** which stretches 24 miles north, across the Canadian border.

A few miles farther, Wash. 20 leaves the park, crossing into lands administered by the **Okanogan National Forest** *(509-996-4000),* where the scenery continues undiminished as you pass through mile after mile of evergreen forest punctuated by burly peaks, dancing creeks, and trailheads. If the call of the wild finally seduces you, there are several fine trails in the vicinity of 4,860-foot **Rainy Pass.** Just before the pass a moderate path goes west 2 miles to **Lake Ann★.** At the

Along the trail to Desolation Peak, above Ross Lake

pass, the flat, paved, and popular **Rainy Lake Trail★** travels a mile to another comely subalpine lake, fed by a waterfall that sluices down from the snowfields above. Four miles east of the pass the moderately steep, 4-mile round-trip **Blue Lake Trail★** leads to yet another heartbreaker of a lake, this one near tree line. Lolling on the rocks overlooking Blue Lake, you may see mountain goats and you're sure to see the jagged pinnacles of 7,600-foot **Liberty Bell Mountain** and the 7,807-foot **Early Winters Spire.** Different views of these peaks can be enjoyed 2 miles up the highway from the Blue Lake trailhead.

Wildflowers, North Cascades National Park

Pass the verdant, rivulet-streaked meadows of **Whistler Basin** to 5,477-foot **Washington Pass★** and pull in at the overlook, which includes a small ranger outpost. Grab an interpretive brochure at the station and hike the quarter-mile loop that ascends to a granite aerie 700 feet above the highway. The panorama is packed with fierce 7,000- and 8,000-foot

Smokejumpers

A call sounds. People rush to a hangar, slip into cumbersome Kevlar suits, put on motorcycle-type helmets fitted with face cages, grab all sorts of gear, and hurry into a small plane—all within ten minutes. Next they fly low over a steep mountainside and parachute into a forest fire, which they fight, working for as long as 24 hours straight. Then they strap on hundred-pound packs and bushwhack to the nearest pickup point. The next day they may do it all over again. This is the life of a smokejumper, and visitors can learn about them a few miles outside Winthrop at the birthplace of smoke jumping: the **North Cascades Smokejumper Base**★ *(Methow Valley State Airport. 509-997-2031. Open during fire season, roughly mid-June to late Sept.).* Off-duty smoke jumpers show visitors their gear, the training area, the planes, and tell hair-raising stories. Of course, if the call comes, your tour guide may suddenly vanish like, well, a puff of smoke.

Fisher Basin, North Cascades National Park

mountains, wind-twisted pines, avalanche chutes, and vertical stone cliffs burnished by glaciers.

From the pass, Wash. 20 descends for some 15 miles through the forest and mountains before it starts to level out in the **Methow Valley**★. Dry-side ponderosa pine, woodlands, and cattle ranches start taking over the landscape. Another 15 miles takes you into the Western-theme town of ❺ **Winthrop** *(Visitor Center 509-996-2125).* The main street area features wooden sidewalks, Old West facades, and even a guitar-toting cowboy strolling about singing western songs. Some will think Winthrop is fun, some will think it's ridiculous, and some will think it's both.

Real Western history can be explored a block beyond downtown Winthrop at the **Shafer Museum** *(285 Castle Ave. 509-996-2712. Daily June-Sept., weekends in May)*. Start at "The Castle," the nickname locals gave to the large log house built in the mid-1890s. From there you can wade amid the artifacts on the grounds and inside the print shop, assay office, and other buildings. Imagine life in the 1889 Nickell's cabin, a 10-by-15-foot place that housed a family of four, and you'll understand how the Castle got its name.

Methow Valley is noted for its outdoor recreation. An easily accessible sample is the **Sun Mountain Trail System★**, which lies a few miles west of Winthrop. The **Beaver Pond Trail** not only passes beaver ponds but meanders through aspen groves and ponderosa stands alive with birds and other wildlife. There's also a nice interpretive trail up by **Sun Mountain Lodge** *(Patterson Lake Rd. 509-996-2211 or 800-572-0493)*, one of the Northwest's most celebrated resorts. Pick up a map and information about the trails in its rustic but elegant lobby. If the expansive views from the dining room don't tempt you to stay for lunch, perhaps the Asian pineapple prawn salad will. Or maybe you'll just decide to spend the night, if there's room and if your bank account is up to it.

To finish the drive, return to Rockport and continue west on Wash. 20. West of ❻ **Concrete,** Baker Lake Road leads north into the popular **Baker Lake** recreation area, which brims with opportunities to hike, fish, camp, and picnic. From there, follow Wash. 20 back to I-5 and go south on the interstate back to Everett.

Downtown Winthrop

Bays to Baker

● 200 miles ● 2 days ● Late spring to early autumn

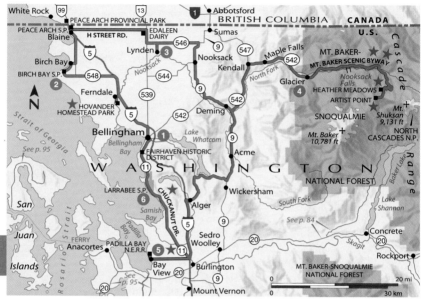

Hovander Homestead horse

How about a stroll on the beach, sorting through seashells and watching cormorants diving in the surf? Or do you feel more like an alpine hike, watching for mountain goats while savoring 10,000-foot peaks? This drive serves up Washington's two most treasured landscapes: the coast and the high Cascades. At its beginning, in Bellingham and nearby Ferndale, it also offers a glimpse of early Northwest history. From there the route leads north into Canada—but only a few hundred yards in, so don't worry about bringing your passport. Compelled by the international boundary, the drive swings east, passing through an outpost of the Netherlands on its way up into the Cascades. From those heights, descend through farms and forest to the coast, returning to Bellingham via scenic Chuckanut Drive.

In 1853 Dirty Dan, who is variously characterized as an entrepreneur or a crook, built a cabin in what is now Bellingham's **Fairhaven Historic District** (*Harris Ave. between 4th and 12th Sts. 360-738-1574*). Dirty Dan has moved on (perhaps up, perhaps down, depending on which characterization was true), but many historic buildings remain. When you're done moseying through the downtown galleries, bookstores, and cafés that now occupy the venerable brick buildings, head up the hill just to the north to look at the many fine old Victorian houses.

The former city hall, a towering 1892 Victorian edifice in downtown ❶ **Bellingham** *(Visitor Center 360-671-3990 or 800-487-2032)*, now contains the **Whatcom Museum of History and Art**★ *(121 Prospect St. 360-676-6981. Closed Mon.)*. As suits a port city, many of the artifacts and works of art have a maritime theme. But this eclectic museum harbors plenty of surprises, such as the extensive exhibit on turn-of-the-century woodworking tools. Next door, the **Whatcom Children's Museum** *(360-733-8769. Closed Mon.; adm. fee)* offers exhibits for the younger set.

The frontier strongly comes to mind 10 miles north in the little town of **Ferndale** *(Chamber of Commerce 360-384-3042)*. At **Pioneer Park** *(1st and Cherry Sts. 360-384-4006. Guided tours mid-May–mid-Sept. Tues.-Sun., park open year-round; fee for tours)*, visitors can peer into more than a dozen original 19th-century buildings, most containing period artifacts. The experience is much richer if you take a tour with one of the docents—you'll know them by their pioneer dress.

A less rustic side of early Ferndale is on view at the **Hovander Homestead Park**★ *(5299 Neilsen Rd. 360-384-3444. House daily June–Labor Day Thurs.-Sun., weekends in May; adm. fee. Grounds and park year-round; adm. fee)*. This large, richly detailed Scandinavian-style home was built at the turn of the century by a wealthy Swedish architect. The grounds hold the **Washington State University Demonstration Garden,** as instructive as it is beautiful. Learn

Where's the Peace Arch?

Straddling Canada and the United States as a symbol of their friendship is the Peace Arch, built in 1921. The beautiful lands, originally purchased through ten-cent contributions from Canadian and American schoolchildren, extend on both sides of the border. By one measure, both arch and gardens lie entirely within Canada, as do long strips of the U.S.—the border is supposed to run along the 49th parallel, but surveyors in the early 1800s miscalculated by about 300 yards. In 1847 both countries agreed the border would always remain where the original survey placed it.

91

Birch Bay State Park, near Ferndale

about cardoon, a cousin to the artichoke, or see how to use copper strips to deter slugs. The huge barn and adjacent pens hold draft horses, geese, potbellied pigs, and more.

Follow your nose to the nearby **Tennant Lake Interpretive Center and Fragrance Garden** ★ *(360-384-3444.*

92

Windmill, Lynden

Center mid-June–Labor Day Thurs.-Sun., boardwalk trail mid-Jan.–mid-Oct., fragrance garden year-round), part of the Hovander Homestead Park complex. The elaborate fragrance garden allows you to make full and glorious use of your sense of smell. Wander along the broad, brick path as it meanders past hundreds of species of aromatic plants. Touch a leaf (it's encouraged), and breathe deeply. Kids love the odor of what one child dubbed the "pizza plant" (oregano). A fine old house serves as the Interpretive Center and natural history museum for the adjacent wetlands. Check out the aquariums and terrariums, which reveal the usually unseen creatures that live in the mud and water of the marsh. To explore the marsh, take the boardwalk trail.

Just north of Ferndale, cut west on Wash. 548 to ❷ **Birch Bay State Park** *(360-371-2800),* a mile-long swath of beachfront forest with some great picnic sites. Continue north to the old-fashioned family resort town of **Birch Bay** *(Chamber of Commerce 360-371-5004).* Another few miles brings you to **Blaine** *(Visitor Center 360-332-4544 or 800-624-3555)* and the Canadian border. DO NOT get caught in the heavy traffic heading up I-5 to the busy border crossing. Instead, drive to **Peace Arch State Park** *(360-332-8221)* and walk into Canada (see sidebar p. 91). The gorgeous flower gardens and the arch itself celebrate the good relations that allow Canada and the United States the luxury of a 3,000-mile, unfortified border.

Leave Blaine via H Street, which parallels the Canadian border. Turn south onto Wash. 539, also known as Guide Meridian Road, and reward yourself with a visit to the **Edaleen Dairy** *(9593 Guide Meridian Rd. 360-354-5342. Closed Sun.).* A local institution, it's usually packed. Pick up an ice-cream cone at the express window—perhaps orange-pineapple macaroon—and watch the cows.

A short drive southeast leads to the tidy, insistently Dutch-style town of ❸ **Lynden** *(Chamber of Commerce 360-354-5995).* Although the Dutch theme may seem overdone, a few establishments do offer genuine glimpses of

Mount Baker Vineyards, Deming

the area's heritage. Also apparent is the strong Calvinistic influence, with a virtual ban on Sunday business. The settler's history can be thoroughly explored at the vast **Lynden Pioneer Museum** *(217 Front St. 360-354-3675. Closed Sun.; adm. fee).*

Drive southeast from Lynden via Wash. 546, 9, and 542 to the town of ❹ **Glacier,** where you should stop at the U.S. Forest Service's **Glacier Public Service Center** *(360-599-2714 in summer, 360-856-5700 rest of year).* Here rangers can provide details and literature about the 24-mile **Mount Baker Scenic Byway**★★, the well-deserved designation given to Wash. 542 east of Glacier. Drive alongside the **North Fork Nooksack River** for 7 miles to Wells Creek Road, where a short spur leads to 175-foot **Nooksack Falls.** About 7 miles farther along the byway, the road begins climbing into the high Cascades, switchbacking more than 3,000 feet in 10 miles.

Stop at **Heather Meadows**★ and nearby **Picture Lake**★ for a stroll amid the wildflowers and heather in the shadow of handsome Mount Shuksan. Trails and the chairlift at nearby **Mount Baker Ski Area** *(360-734-6771)* offer access to even higher elevations and top-of-the-world views. When the snow is gone, in midsummer and early fall, travelers can also drive to summit-like vistas by going the last few miles to the end of the road at **Artist Point**★ and enjoy a hike along the easy, mile-long **Artist Ridge Trail**★★, one of the most scenic hikes in the Northwest.

Make your way back down the byway and out Wash. 542 to southbound Wash. 9. After a pleasant 15 minutes through the bucolic countryside, turn onto Park Drive, which

Picture Lake and Mount Shuksan

becomes South Bay Drive as it runs into **Lake Whatcom,** a 15-mile-long, evergreen-lined beauty. Continue on to Cain Lake Road, which goes to Alger and I-5. From here, the route heads south for 9 miles to meet up with Wash. 11.

But before starting up Wash. 11, travel 5 miles due west on Josh Wilson Road to Padilla Bay. Just north on the coast is the Interpretive Center of ❺ **Padilla Bay National Estuarine Research Reserve**★ *(1043 Bayview-Edison Rd. 360-428-1558. Wed.-Sun.),* where aquariums, displays, and hands-on exhibits teach about hairy sea squirts, spiny lumpsuckers, and the other, more familiar denizens of Padilla Bay. Shoreline and upland interpretive trails give hikers a firsthand look at the estuary.

Back on Wash. 11, you'll soon realize that this scenic road deserves more than an impersonal number. Indeed, locals long ago gave it a name: **Chuckanut Drive**★. Built in 1896, this was the first road to connect Whatcom County with points south. Ten of its 20 miles tightrope above **Samish Bay,** looking across the water to Rosario Strait and the San Juan Islands. Midway lies ❻ **Larrabee State Park** *(360-676-2093),* where trails lead down to a popular beach and along the rims of the coastal bluffs to more secluded coves. A few miles north the route returns to Bellingham.

Farmland near Bellingham, Mount Baker in the distance

Washington's Waterfront ★★

- 185 miles ● 3 to 4 days ● Spring through autumn
- Plan your itinerary around the five ferry routes that connect this drive (see sidebar p. 102).

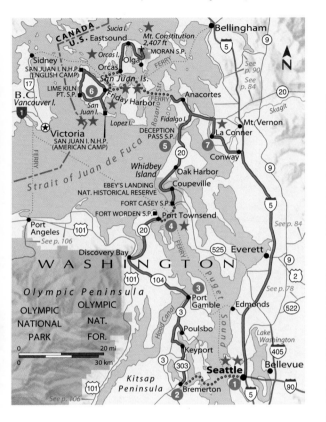

See p. 90
See p. 84
See p. 84
See p. 106
See p. 78
See p. 106

Chinatown/International District

Neither "Chinatown" nor "International District" quite captures the nature of this vibrant neighborhood on the southern edge of downtown Seattle. It's essentially Asian, comprising Chinese, Japanese, Koreans, and Vietnamese, and was historically also an African-American community. The district's past comes to light at the **Wing Luke Asian Museum** ★ (407 7th Ave. S. 206-623-5124. Closed Mon.; adm. fee), dedicated to the culture, history, and art of Asian-Pacific Americans. The present is evident at **Uwajimaya** (519 6th Ave. S. 206-624-6248), the ever lively Asian superstore that includes a deli, bookstore, and gift shop. Enjoy!

Via road and ferry, this route makes ports of call throughout the jigsaw puzzle of islands and peninsulas that characterize the Puget Sound region. A notably varied drive, it includes the metropolitan amenities of Seattle, the naval culture of Kitsap Peninsula, the Victorian charm of historic Port Townsend, small towns nuzzled by deep blue waters, and miles of forested coves and islands.

Begin in ❶ **Seattle** ★★ (Visitor Center 206-461-5840), a metropolis of 1.5 million. Although urban sprawl and thick traffic detract from its celebrated natural setting, this remains a handsome and vibrant city. Take your cue from Seattle's founding settlers and begin at the **waterfront** ★, the recreational waterfront, that is. This 1.5-mile stretch along **Elliott Bay** lies at the foot of downtown and holds shops, restaurants, parks, ferry docks, boat tour operators,

and piers barnacled with businesses. On Pier 59, get
a preview of the drive beyond Seattle by visiting Puget
Sound habitats and a working salmon ladder at the
Seattle Aquarium *(206-386-4320. Adm. fee).*

Seattle also harbors one of the nation's largest working
waterfronts, a prime port in the booming Pacific Rim trade.

Seattle skyline

No tramp freighters here; Seattle's cargo terminals feature
skyscraper-size cranes hoisting containers on and off
colossal modern ships. Several viewpoints invite you to see
the international marketplace in action. The best overall
vista comes through the observation deck telescopes at the
conference center at the new **Bell Street Pier Complex**
on Pier 66. The Port of Seattle also operates one of the
North Pacific's largest commercial fishing harbors, **Fishermen's Terminal** *(1735 W. Thurman St. 206-728-3000).*

Several of Seattle's prime attractions lie just beyond the
waterfront. One, arguably the city's most beloved, is **Pike
Place Market**★★ *(Bounded by Western Ave., Virginia St., 1st
Ave., and just S of Pike St. 206-682-7453).* Founded in 1907
when outraged housewives campaigned to remove
price-gouging middlemen, the market has grown enormous
(4 city blocks and then some), but has largely avoided
becoming a tourist trap or upscale enclave. Fishmongers

still hurl fresh salmon across walkways, perhaps a hundred farmers still bring in all manner of produce, and working stiffs (and savvy visitors) can still get a cheap, decent meal and a millionaire's view at some of the cafés.

A few blocks away, the **Seattle Art Museum**★ *(100 University St. 206-654-3100. Closed Mon.; adm. fee)* convincingly demonstrates that man doth not live by bread alone. Before rushing in to contemplate the large, eclectic collection, pause to admire the striking 1991 building and the towering "Hammering Man" piece by Jonathan Borofsky.

Pioneer Square adjoins the waterfront to the south. Here in the early 1850s Seattle was born on the mudflats of Elliott Bay. After the great 1889 fire, the city rebuilt above the mud, leaving an underground labyrinth below. Some of that subterranean realm can be toured via **Bill Speidel's Underground Tour** *(610 1st Ave. 206-682-4646 or 800-60-UNDER. Adm. fee)*. The guides give a light-hearted history of that pre-fire era, much of which was dominated by Henry Yesler, timber baron and Seattle's first mayor. Proof that political corruption is nothing new, Yesler paved Seattle's streets—but only as far as his house. He also instituted the county's first lottery, which he happened to win. Above ground, many of the (nonflammable) brick edifices built after the 1889 fire still grace this historic district. Now they house a large concentration of the city's finest art galleries, a variety of nightclubs, restaurants by the dozen, the **Klondike Gold Rush National Historic Park** *(117 S. Main St. 206-553-7220),* and Seattle's acclaimed bookstore and literary hangout, the **Elliott Bay Book Company**★ *(101 S. Main St. 206-624-6600).* Visitors share Pioneer Square with the full range of Seattle society, from wealthy art patrons and famous authors to grunge rockers and street people.

Fishmongers, Pike Place Market

A few blocks north towers Seattle's definitive modern landmark, the **Space Needle** *(5th Ave. and Broad St. 206-443-2111 or 800-937-9382. Adm. fee).* For an overpriced but impressive view, head to the restaurant or observation deck atop this 605-foot symbol of the 1962 World's Fair.

97

More importantly, the needle marks the location of **Seattle Center**★ *(206-684-7200),* the 74-acre park brimming with attractions, including the **Seattle Symphony Orchestra** *(206-443-4747. Adm. fee),* the **Seattle Children's Museum** *(206-441-1768. Adm. fee),* **Key Arena,** the **Pacific Northwest Ballet** *(206-441-9411. Adm. fee),* and the **Intiman Theatre Company** *(206-269-1900. Adm. fee).* If you have kids or an interest in science, allow a half day for the fabulous **Pacific Science Center**★ ★ *(200 2nd Ave. N. 206-443-2001. Adm. fee);* if you have both, take a full day. The five cavernous buildings house thousands of exhibits, many of the hands-on variety. Check out the planetarium, operate the life-size jaws of a *T. rex,* play virtual basketball, search for the queen of the naked mole rats, or see an IMAX film.

Another half-day to all-day visit for travelers with kids and an interest in science is the **Woodland Park Zoo**★ ★ *(5500 Phinney Ave. N. 206-684-4800. Adm. fee).* Simply put, it's one of the world's top zoos. About 20 years ago it started the trend that is transforming zoos worldwide, by putting animals in areas that mimic their natural habitats, encouraging the animals to behave naturally. The male and female siamangs (a species of gibbon from Sumatra) inflate their volleyball-size throat pouches and howl, moan, sing, and chatter their blaring duets. A giraffe sticks out its foot-long tongue to reach high into a tree for new leaves—touring the zoo can feel like moving from one region of the world to another.

When you're finally ready to leave Seattle, return to the waterfront and board the ferry *(Pier 52. 206-464-6400 or 800-84-FERRY. Fare)* for the hour run to ❷ **Bremerton** *(Chamber of Commerce 360-479-3579).* It's appropriate to arrive by water, as Bremerton has been a Navy town since its shipyard was founded more than a hundred years ago. Visitors can soak up some of this naval atmosphere, past and present, in the area near the ferry terminal. A block up the hill lies the **Bremerton Naval Museum** *(130 Washington Ave.*

Adventuress on Puget Sound

98

360-479-7447. Closed Mon. Labor Day–Mem. Day; donation). Artifacts, photos, and models tell the history of the U.S. Navy, with a logical emphasis on Bremerton's shipyard.

Down on the boardwalk, landlubbers can imagine a sailor's life by touring a decommissioned destroyer, the **U.S.S. *Turner Joy*** *(300 Washington Beach Ave. 360-792-2457. Closed Tues.-Wed. Oct.–mid-May; adm. fee).* From the bridge and the torpedo launchers to the precipitous ladders and closet-size barber shop, most of the 1959 ship is in its original condition. A tour boat leaves from this site for a 45-minute cruise to look at the **Puget Sound Naval Shipyard** and the **Mothball Fleet** *(Kipsap Harbor Tours, 290 Washington Beach Ave. 360-377-8924. Daily mid-May–Sept., weekends rest of year; adm. fee).* Passengers can see dozens of active and decommissioned vessels, from submarines to battleships. Among them (when it's in port) may be the world's largest warship, the 1,092-foot supercarrier **U.S.S. *Nimitz.*** The guide explains that the *Nimitz* carries a crew of 5,500, 100 planes, and packs more firepower than was released by all forces during World War II.

The naval theme continues some 15 miles north in **Keyport** at the **Naval Undersea Museum** ★ *(Garnett Way. 360-396-4148. Closed Tues. Oct.-May).* As one would expect, the museum includes extensive exhibits on submarines and torpedoes, but much of the information and artifacts are surprising. For example, the first successful submarine, the *American Turtle,* was built of wood in 1776. The excellent exhibits, many hands-on, illuminate elements of the ocean environment, such as salinity, pressure, density, and buoyancy. Also on the grounds is the sail of the fast attack submarine U.S.S. *Sturgeon.*

Naval Undersea Museum, Keyport

For a decidedly nonmilitary ambience, drive to the other side of Liberty Bay to **Poulsbo** *(360-779-4848),* a town known for its Norwegian heritage. Its self-consciously cute **Old Town** teems with shops, galleries, cafés, and tourists, and at its southern end, on the bay, lies the **Marine Science Center** *(18743 Front St. N.E. 360-779-5549. Adm. fee).* It's small and informal, with about ten touch tanks that allow you to see and (appropriately) handle rubber-spiked sea cucumbers, sea anemones, and other Puget Sound denizens.

A ten-minute drive north leads back a century at ❸ **Port**

Gamble *(Visitor Center 360-297-8200 or 800-416-5616),* a small, tidy village founded in 1853. It was built by timber giant Pope & Talbot as a company town, and Pope Resources still owns and maintains the townsite, now a historic district. Many buildings date back to the 19th century.

Tide pooling, Deception Pass State Park

Above the classic old general store you'll find the **Of Sea & Shore Museum** *(1 Rainier Ave. 360-297-2426. Closed Mon. mid-May–mid-Sept., weekends only mid-Sept.–mid-May; donation),* featuring a large collection of seashells and marine life. The **Port Gamble Historical Museum** *(Behind the general store. 360-297-8074. Mem. Day–Labor Day; adm. fee)* exhibits items from the early days of the timber industry and Port Gamble.

For a taste of the **Olympic Peninsula** (see Olympic Peninsula drive, p. 106), take Wash. 104 across **Hood Canal,** a beautiful, natural body of water, despite its name. Follow Wash. 20 to the waterfront town of ❹ **Port Townsend**★ *(Visitor Center 360-385-2722),* and one of the most extensive and well-preserved

San Juan Islands

historic districts in the Northwest *(for walking tours, call 360-385-4356 or 360-385-1967).* Dozens of elaborate 19th-century brick buildings adorn the downtown, and an even greater number of fancy Victorian homes dot the residential streets. The old city hall now holds the **Jefferson County Historical Society Museum** *(210 Madison St. 360-385-1003. Adm. fee)*, a four-story grandma's attic awash in the past. Nearby, **Fort Worden State Park** *(360-385-4730)* houses a grab bag of tenants, including the **Coast Artillery Museum** *(360-385-0373. Mid-May–Aug., weekends rest of year; adm. fee)* and the **Port Townsend Marine Science Center** *(360-385-5582. Mid-June–Oct. Tues.-Sun., weekends rest of year; adm. fee)*, as well as the buildings and gun emplacements from its years defending Puget Sound from a naval invasion.

Ferry to **Whidbey Island** *(Island County Tourism 360-675-3535 or 888-747-7777)*, one of the largest islands in the lower 48, and dock right below **Fort Casey State Park** *(360-678-4519)*, one of Fort Worden's two counterparts. The artillery batteries are better preserved here than at Fort Worden, with some of the big guns still in place. Check out the **Admiralty Head Lighthouse Interpretive Center** *(360-679-7391. April-Sept. Thurs.-Sun., call for off-season hours)*, which offers exhibits and big views of the Olympic Mountains. Next, head to the little town of **Coupeville**— the small farms, woodlands, and beaches of this central

island region have remained relatively unchanged since the 19th century—and pick up a map for 17,400-acre **Ebey's Landing National Historical Reserve** *(Island County Historical Society Museum, Front and Alexander Sts. 360-678-3310.*

Ferry Survival

Much about ferry travel is idyllic, but it is not without hard realities. **Washington State Ferries** (206-464-6400 or 800-84-FERRY. Fare) is among the largest ferry systems in the nation; its 24 ferries haul 24 million passengers a year. And there are no reservations unless travelers are going to Canada (though plans for a reservation system in the San Juans are being discussed). To avoid long waits, travel early or travel late, unless it's a commuter route; then go in the middle of the day. Travel between Anacortes and the San Juans is very heavy on sunny weekends and during summer; bring a long book, as you may wait several hours. Because ferries vary so much, it's wise to ask the locals or the ferry information folks how to best cope with a particular route.

Closed Tues.-Thurs. Oct.-April, reserve open year-round).

Go north on Wash. 20, but before crossing the bridge to Fidalgo Island, tarry in the southern portion of ❺ **Deception Pass State Park** *(360-675-2417).* This is Washington's most popular state park; in summer you'll have to share the 4,600 acres of trails, driftwood-strewn beaches, and lakes. If you enjoy vertigo, walk to the center of the Deception Pass Bridge that spans the narrows between the islands and stare down as the tide surges through.

Continue about 10 miles across Fidalgo Island to the Anacortes Ferry *(fare).* As the ferry pushes away from land, prepare to be transported in more than the literal sense. Within minutes you'll be meandering through the **San Juan Islands★★,** so set your watch to island time—take it off. Disembark at **Friday Harbor★,** the only incorporated city on ❻ **San Juan Island★★** *(Visitor Information 360-468-3663 or Chamber of Commerce 360-378-5240).* Some islanders disavow this busy town of shops, restaurants, and hostelries, but visitors are likely to find something of interest. For starters, stop at **The Whale Museum** *(62 1st St. N. 360-378-4710. Closed Tues. Oct.–Mem. Day; adm. fee).* San Juan residents are gaga over whales, especially the orcas that patrol local waters; you can't swing a stick inside a gift shop without hitting a stuffed killer whale or an orca mug. You'll begin to understand the islanders' passion as you peruse the museum. Did you know that blue whale babies are the fastest growing of all mammals, gaining nine pounds an hour? Or that "auntie" whales help deliver and protect newborns, and even tried to lead whaling ships away from calves? If you really want to fall for whales, stand inside the converted phone booth and listen to their songs.

Some worthwhile galleries lurk amid the town's many gift shops. To continue the whale theme, walk two orca-lengths down from the museum to **Whalesong** *(20 First St. 360-378-6722).* This gallery features the striking whale photos of Kelley Balcomb-Bartok, a local man who grew up around whales; his father runs the island's Center for Whale Research and is a leading authority on orcas. Or try **Island Studios** *(270 Spring St. 360-378-6550. Closed Sun.-Tues. Jan.-Feb.),* which displays the work of about a hundred local artists, most several cuts above the usual seascapes and pottery.

Beyond Friday Harbor stretches a 15-by-8.75-mile island of forest and field, dotted with parks, small farms, some houses, a venerable resort, marinas, and a wealth of snug coves. At either end lie the opposing camps of the Pig War. **San Juan Island National Historical Park**

(360-378-2240) comprises two units: **English Camp** *(West Valley Rd.)* and **American Camp** *(Cattle Point Rd.)*. Tension over which country owned the island escalated into serious saber-rattling after an American settler shot a trespassing British pig. Thousands of troops and several warships bristled at one another until saner people arrived, including a high-ranking British admiral who asserted that he would not "involve two great nations in a war over a squabble about a pig." In addition to historic buildings and information about the Pig War, the park, especially American Camp, features some nice hiking trails.

Those cherished orcas can sometimes be spotted off the west coast. Docents, interpretive signs, and vantage points from the rocky shoreline draw whale-watchers to **Lime Kiln Point State Park** *(6158 Lighthouse Rd. 360-378-2044)*. From May to the beginning of August, one of three resident pods of orcas will spend much of its time in this area feeding on salmon. But you should consider yourself lucky if you see one of these pods of killer whales at all.

The odds of seeing orcas increase sharply for those who venture out on one of the whale-watching boats *(for information call Visitor Information. Most boats run April-Oct.; fare)* based in Friday Harbor; their success rate exceeds 90 percent in May and June and stays above 50 percent in late April and from July through mid-October. Shop around for an operator who features longer trips (four hours or so), onboard naturalists, and who belongs to the Whale Watching Operators Association Northwest, which trains members to watch whales without harassing them. The better operators also pay attention to other aspects of the islands' natural history, such as the nesting bald eagles, the harbor seals that pup on some of the islets in early July, and the Dall's porpoises that bound through the water like antelope. But the orcas remain the headliners, and for good reason. Not only are these up-to-30-foot, black-and-white members of the dolphin family strikingly handsome, highly social,

Tulip fields, Skagit Valley

communicative, fierce and crafty predators; they're also great fun to watch. Passengers sometimes will see orcas launch out of the water (breaching), slap the surface with their flippers or tails (tailslapping), and poke their heads straight up out of the water (spyhopping).

As you search for orcas, notice that the San Juans consist of dozens of islands—hundreds if you count all the little fellas. So many possibilities, though the state ferries serve only San Juan and the three other big and relatively populous islands. (A number of small, private craft can get you out to the backwaters.) Sample another island by stopping on **Orcas Island**★ *(Visitor Information 360-468-3663)*, about a 45-minute ferry ride northeast of Friday Harbor.

Sucia Island, with Mount Baker in background

104

This large, hilly island of forests, sheep pastures, and hamlets tempts motorists with many miles of scenic drives, backroads every one. One snakes to the top of **Mount Constitution**★ in **Moran State Park** *(360-376-2326)*, a 2,407-foot summit that presents one of the best views in the Pacific Northwest. From the top rampart of an old stone tower *(road often closed in winter)* you behold a panorama of the San Juans, the neighboring Gulf Islands in Canada, southern Vancouver Island, the Olympic Peninsula, and vast chunks of the mainlands of British Columbia and Washington.

Motorists also should stop in **Eastsound** *(Visitor Information 360-468-3663)* to lunch at one of the bayside cafés, admire the pretty little 1885 church, or browse a handful of galleries—the San Juans are positively crawling with artists. A few hundred

yards from town, down the sound's east shore, lies
Madrona Point, a park that gets its name from the
thousands of red-and-orange-barked Pacific madrone
trees that shade the maze of hiking trails. To glimpse the
richness of local waters, explore the rocks and tide pools
along the park shore; they teem with crabs of many
species, sea stars by the hundreds, and horse clams that
squirt water 5 feet in the air as you approach their hiding
places in the sand.

Roll off the ferry back in Anacortes and head about
9 miles east on Wash. 20. Then hit the brakes and go
south on Whitney-La Conner Road to ❼ **La Conner**★
(Chamber of Commerce 360-466-4778). This small town was
plotted in the mid-1800s as a shipping port along the
Swinomish Channel. The town's main drag still lies along
the channel, where dozens of restaurants, shops, hostelries,
and galleries now inhabit many of the original buildings.
During the summer tourists crowd First Street, but don't
let that prevent you from sampling this downtown's con-
siderable charms, especially its art offerings.

First tour the bright, spacious **Museum of Northwest
Art** *(121 S. 1st St. 360-466-4446. Closed Mon.; adm. fee),* which
opened in 1995; don't miss the space devoted to glass
works. Then browse some of First Street's many fine
galleries, which, in a welcome departure from the typical
tourist strip, far outnumber the souvenir shops. Unusual
galleries include **The Wood Merchant** *(709 S. 1st St. 360-
466-4741),* which carries some exquisite wooden furniture, sculpture, jewelry boxes, and rocking chairs; and
Caravan Gallery *(619 S. 1st St. 360-466-4808),* which offers
New Guinea masks, Tuareg (northwestern Africa) swords,
jewelry, leather amulet boxes, and other exotic works in a
museumlike setting. You'll notice a number of old, well-
kept buildings; historic edifices pepper La Conner. Perhaps
the finest is the 1891 **Gaches Mansion** *(703 S. 2nd St. 360-
466-4288. March-Dec. Fri.-Sun.; adm. fee).* Artifacts from the
early days can be viewed at the **Skagit County Historical
Museum** *(501 4th St. 360-466-3365. Closed Mon.; adm. fee).*
Simply wander the pleasant neighborhoods behind the
main drag and you'll encounter many worthy old houses.
You'll also find your pace slowing as you savor the La
Conner beloved by its citizens.

Assuming you resist the common temptation to buy a
house and move here, drive southeast through the **Skagit
Delta.** If it's springtime the farm fields will blaze with
flowering bulbs, the Skagit Delta's most famous crop. At
Conway, get onto I-5 and head back to Seattle.

105

Olympic Peninsula★★

● **335 miles** ● **3 to 4 days** ● **Spring through autumn**

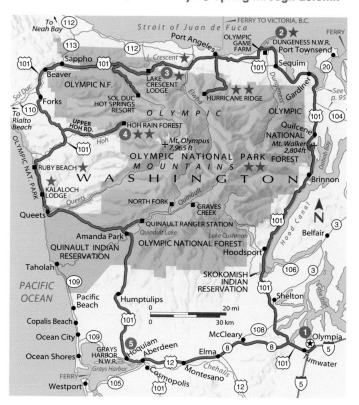

Cruising the three coasts of the Olympic Peninsula allows travelers to taste many savory sites: a seaworthy replica of a historic sailing ship; a bustling Pacific Rim port; a wildlife-rich sand spit that thrusts 5 miles out into the Strait of Juan de Fuca; and a sunny valley of berry patches and small farms. But, like a chocolate-covered cherry, the heart of the matter lies in the center—in this case Olympic National Park. The drive skirts the edges of the peninsula because the park's jagged mountains, conifer forest, and wealth of rivers and lakes block its middle. Spur roads lead back to alpine meadows frequented by marmots and black bears, hot springs, old-growth forest where elk walk beneath 300-foot trees, and mountain summits that yield top-of-the-world panoramas.

Those who recall their geography know the small city of ❶ **Olympia** *(Visitor Center 360-753-8447)* as the capital of Washington. Its **Capitol Campus** ★ *(Capitol Information Center 360-586-3460)* is one of the most beautiful in the nation. Set on a bluff overlooking the waters of Puget Sound, the 28-story domed **Legislative Building**★ brims with rich detail, such as decorative plaster ceilings alive with eagles and Louis Tiffany's five-ton "Angels of Mercy" chandelier. The surrounding campus also contains groves of Japanese cherry trees, a botanical conservatory, a reproduction of a fountain from Denmark's Tivoli Gardens, an English-style sunken garden, and the governor's mansion. Olympia's history, particularly its struggle to become the state capital, is recounted at the **State Capital Museum** *(211 W. 21st Ave. 360-753-2580. Closed Mon.; adm. fee),* housed in the 32-room Lord Mansion.

Olympic Game Farm, Sequim

About 30 miles north, US 101 cozies up to the west bank of **Hood Canal,** a pretty, natural waterway, its name notwithstanding. For another 30 miles or so, the drive curves along the water, encountering oyster farms, marshes replete with wildlife, and small towns offering good clam chowder with a view. For a surpassing vista, turn off on Forest Road 2730 and drive 4 miles to the 2,804-foot summit of **Mount Walker,** from which you can see sights from Mount Baker and Mount Rainier to the Space Needle in Seattle.

Shortly after US 101 makes the bend and starts running west along the **Strait of Juan de Fuca** comes the pastoral **Dungeness Valley,** sandwiched between the strait and the snowy peaks of the Olympic Mountains. In addition to providing a scenic backdrop for dairy cows and berry farms, those mountains cast a rain shadow across the sunny valley, which receives only 17 inches a year.

Along the valley's scenic loop is the ❷ **Dungeness National Wildlife Refuge**★ *(360-457-8451. Adm. fee).* Its main feature is a 5.5-mile sand spit that hooks out into the strait to an old lighthouse. During spring and fall thousands of waterfowl and shorebirds descend on the shallow waters protected by the spit, and people hiking along it can see bald eagles, great blue herons, loons, and harbor seals.

About 15 miles west of the Dunge-

107

Strait of Juan de Fuca, from Dungeness Spit

ness Valley, US 101 rolls into **Port Angeles** *(Chamber of Commerce 360-452-2363).* As the name suggests, the action is down at the port. From atop the observation tower on the **City Pier** *(Foot of Lincoln St.),* visitors can see huge ships gorging on logs for export; the paper, pulp, and plywood mills that line the harbor; the tankers and cargo ships plying the shipping lanes in the strait; and, in the background, Vancouver Island to the north and the Olympic Mountains to the south. Also on the pier is the **Arthur D. Feiro Marine Lab**★ *(360-417-6254. Daily mid-June–mid-Sept., weekends rest of year; adm. fee).* This small but excellent facility teaches about life in the region's ocean waters. Plenty of friendly docents provide insight into the world of sea cucumbers, sea anemones, giant Pacific octopuses, and sea slugs—there's even a chance to gently handle some critters.

Bring those background mountains into the foreground and head south on Hurricane Ridge Road into a few of the 922,000 acres that comprise **Olympic National Park**★ ★ *(Visitor Center in Port Angeles 360-452-0330. Adm. fee for park).* The paved road winds up over 5,000 feet to **Hurricane Ridge**★ ★, a justifiably popular mountain citadel that puts visitors at the edge of the park's exceptionally jagged peaks. Several fine trails fan out from here, but don't miss the 3-mile round-trip **Hurricane Hill Trail**★ ★ (it gets crowded, so start early in the day). The grade is steep, but that's all right, because you'll want to stop to admire the brilliant wildflowers that throng the meadows in summer. Watch for wildlife, too; Olympic marmots and black-tailed deer often show up, and black bear are fairly common. From the meadows at the summit visitors get a superb 360-degree view that embraces the surrounding mountains, the strait, the San Juan Islands, a chunk of mainland Washington, and a fair bit of Canada.

Back in Port Angeles, continue west on US 101 for some 15 miles to **Lake Crescent**★, where you once again enter Olympic National Park. For the next several

Wildflowers along Hurricane Hill Trail, Olympic National Park

miles US 101 adheres to the south shore of this long, deep, glacial lake. Many pullouts invite picnics or prolonged gazing at the lake and the encircling forest and mountains.

Traditional dance performance, Neah Bay Center

About halfway along the shoreline, you can turn off and ease through the towering firs and hemlocks to historic ❸ **Lake Crescent Lodge**★ (*360-928-3211. Late April–late Oct.*), a nice place to lunch while looking out upon the lake. Not far away travelers can hike a mile up to 90-foot **Marymere Falls**★.

A few miles west of Lake Crescent, just inside the park's boundary, take a scenic 12-mile trip south along the beautifully forested **Sol Duc River** to **Sol Duc Hot Springs Resort** (*360-327-3583. Mid-May–mid-Sept.; adm. fee*). The main attraction is the 130-degree mineral water; don't worry, it's cooled through a heat exchanger to keep temperatures in the three hot pools tolerable. Several trails branch out from here, notably the path following the Sol Duc River for a mile out through towering old-growth forest to **Sol Duc Falls**★, a triple cascade that tumbles some 60 feet into a dizzyingly narrow chasm.

From the Sol Duc, take US 101 west and then south to the definitive timber town of **Forks** (*Visitor Center 360-374-2531 or 800-44FORKS*) and the **Forks Timber Museum** (*South edge of town on US 101. 360-374-9663. Mid-April–Oct. and by appt.*). Its displays on the peninsula's timber industry give travelers a historical perspective of the region.

About 12 miles from Forks, turn east on Upper Hoh Road and drive back into Olympic National Park and the ❹ **Hoh Rain Forest**★★. Rain forests are rare in temperate zones. To see what 140 inches of annual rainfall

Makah Museum★

In 1970 coastal erosion near the Makah village of Ozette exposed a cluster of well-preserved 500-year-old houses that had sheltered some of the tribe's ancestors. The thousands of artifacts recovered were used to create the **Makah Museum** (*Wash. 112. 360-645-2711. Closed Mon.-Tues. mid-Sept.–May; adm. fee*), located in Neah Bay on the Makah Reservation. Visitors can see hunting materials, abalone jewelry, as well as replicas of a longhouse and a 30-foot cedar canoe that Makah men used for whaling.

creates, walk the 0.75-mile **Hall of Mosses Trail★★.** Overhead spreads a canopy of spruce, hemlock, and fir, some nearly 300 feet tall. The understory is a green riot of vine maple, red alder, and sorrel. Moss, lichens, and ferns seem to sprout everywhere, virtually encasing some trees. The light even turns a bit green as it filters through this abundant realm. The **Spruce Nature Trail★★,** a 1.25-mile loop, leads through similarly verdant forest down to the Hoh River, where Roosevelt elk are sometimes seen. To learn more, stop by the **Hoh Rain Forest Visitor Center** *(360-452-0330. Call for hours).*

Seagull, Rialto Beach

Return to US 101 and follow it along the Hoh River down to the southernmost section of Olympic National Park's coastal unit. The highway joins the shore at **Ruby Beach★** and paces the sea for about 10 miles, providing access to numerous sandy beaches, rocky coves, forested bluffs, and cliff-top viewpoints. About 7 miles south, you can stop for lunch at the venerable **Kalaloch Lodge★** *(360-962-2271),* and enjoy the view overlooking the ocean.

Several miles south, US 101 turns inland and heads back into the forest, or what's left of it in this heavily logged area. About 25 miles out of Kalaloch, the highway comes to **Quinault Lake** and the southern part of the national park. Take the road along the north shore of the

Rialto Beach, near La Push, Olympic National Park

lake up to the ranger station and you once again can stroll amid the big trees on the 0.5-mile **Maple Glade Rain Forest Trail★.** If that only whets your appetite for old-growth forest, continue east up the **Quinault River Valley★★** to the trails out of North Fork or Graves Creek.

From Quinault Lake drive south on US 101 about 40 miles to **Grays Harbor.** Just west on Wash. 109 from ➎ **Hoquiam** lies the **Grays Harbor National Wildlife Refuge** *(360-532-6237 or 360-753-9467).* The refuge shelters a variety of wildlife, but the stars are the shorebirds. You are likely to see thousands, and in spring up to half a million, of shorebirds of two dozen species that frequent the productive mudflats to feed and rest before flying to their northern breeding grounds.

In Hoquiam, check out the extravagant **Hoquiam's Castle** *(515 Chenault Ave. 360-533-2005. Daily June-Aug., weekends Sept.-Nov. and Jan.-May; adm. fee)*, built by a timber tycoon in 1897. Don't miss the incongruously tacky saloon on the third floor. Also in town is the **Arnold Polson Museum** *(1611 Riverside Ave. 360-533-5862. June–Labor Day Wed.-Sun., Sept.-May Sat.-Sun.; adm. fee)*, another mansion paid for by timber money. This 26-room house now holds extensive displays on the history of the area.

Take US 101 4 miles east to **Aberdeen** *(Chamber of Commerce 360-532-1924)* and wander through **Grays Harbor Historical Seaport** *(360-532-8611. Tour fee)*. The seaport's highlight is the meticulously crafted replica of the ***Lady Washington***★, the tall ship that Capt. Robert Gray sailed into these waters in 1788 and the first American vessel to land in the Pacific Northwest. This seaworthy ship sometimes ventures out to sea, so check to see if it's in port when you are. From Aberdeen, take US 12 and Wash. 8 back to Olympia.

Ruby Beach, Olympic National Park

Around Mount Rainier ★

● **200 miles** ● **3 days** ● **Early summer to early autumn** ● **Snow typically closes the high parts of the loop from mid-October to early June. No gas available in Mount Rainier National Park.**

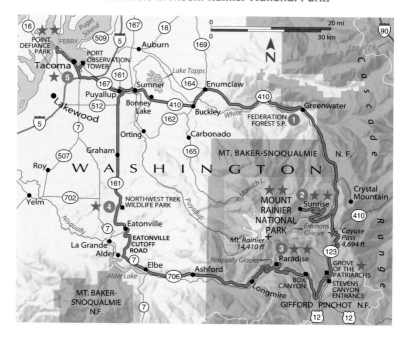

Mount Rainier serves as this drive's hub, seldom out of view as you make a big circle around the 14,410-foot peak. The Northwest's highest mountain anchors a beautiful national park replete with old-growth forests, flowery subalpine meadows, and rivers born from the glaciers

Mount Rainier, from Paradise

that streak the peak's upper slopes. The nature theme continues outside the park at a wildlife park and in the surrounding national forests and designated wilderness areas, with Tacoma providing the urban note.

Though 70 miles away from Tacoma (see p. 116), where the drive begins, **Mount Rainier** rules the horizon, beckoning. Why resist? Give in and drive southeast on Wash. 167 and 410. You'll soon pick up the **White River,** which you can follow right up to the glaciers on Mount Rainier's northeast flank. Stop at ❶ **Federation Forest State Park** *(40 miles E of Tacoma, just W of Greenwater. 360-663-2207. Early May–late Oct. or by appt.),* where a modest but well-conceived Interpretive Center provides an introduction to the state's main ecological zones, and two trails thick with informative signs lead through the forest and along the river.

About 15 minutes south on Wash. 410 lies the northeast boundary of **Mount Rainier National Park★★** *(360-569-2211. Some areas open year-round, others seasonal; adm. fee).* Five miles into the park, take the winding road leading west up to ❷ **Sunrise★★,** the highest point in the park accessible by car (6,400 feet). Allow plenty of time to make your way up the 16-mile spur; not only is the road serpentine, but trails, a campground, and viewpoints may waylay you. For example, the **Glacier Basin Trail★** leads from the White River Campground to a close view of **Emmons Glacier,** the largest glacier in the lower 48 states.

Upon reaching the end of this road, the first order of business is to gape at the looming mountain. Then it's time to hike Sunrise's extensive trail system. For grand views reaching as far as the Canadian mountains 150 miles away, troop up the moderately demanding **Burroughs**

No Meadow Stomping

After his 1888 visit to what is now the Paradise area of Mount Rainier, John Muir wrote, "Every one of these parks [meadows], great and small, is a garden filled knee-deep with fresh, lovely flowers of every hue, the most luxuriant and the most extravagantly beautiful of all the alpine gardens I have beheld." Unfortunately, such beauty drew many visitors and the fragile subalpine meadows were damaged by boots, tents, and horses' hooves. Some people even set subalpine firs on fire because the exploding sap made pretty "fireworks," and a desire for fresh milk led to cows grazing on the meadows. These egregious abuses have stopped, but visitors walking off trails still cause extensive and long-lasting damage. Heed the signs and buttons that read, "Don't Be A Meadow Stomper. Stay On Trails."

113

Mountain Trail★ or **Mount Fremont Trail**★ through alpine tundra, an Arctic-like habitat of rocks and low-growing plants. Scan the ground for hoary marmots, plump, woodchuck-looking rodents that emit shrill whistles. Keep an eye open for mountain goats on the steep slopes, those white-haired, goateed climbers par excellence. Human climbers may also be visible on the mountain's icy inclines.

Continue down Wash. 410 until Cayuse Pass, then take Wash. 123 south (Wash. 410 takes a sharp turn east). Follow this for 11 miles through stream-laced forests to the Stevens Canyon Entrance, then turn west onto the road that traverses the southern expanse of the park. You'll soon arrive at the trailhead to the **Grove of the Patriarchs**★. An easy walk of less than a mile (one way) along the **Ohanapecosh River** leads to the grove of old-growth trees that tower above an island in the river and give the trail its name. Cross the bridge, stroll beneath their mossy, gnarled limbs, and touch the rough, deeply furrowed bark of their massive trunks, some a good 10 feet in diameter. Many of these ancient Douglas-firs and western red cedars were around before Columbus sailed in 1492; a few sprouted more than a thousand years ago. Signs tell how these old ones avoided and survived fire, flood, and disease. To see a younger, more vital old-growth forest of great beauty, go back over the bridge and branch off to the north on the **East Side Trail**★. Sample a mile or so of this lush forest or, if you're feeling energetic, hike its full length back to the Cayuse Pass area.

To the west, numerous viewpoints and trails invite lingering as the road eases through untouched forest, passing rugged ridges, creeks, and peaks. An easy, half-mile walk from the **Box Canyon/Muddy Fork Cowlitz** bridge shows off a dizzyingly deep and narrow river gorge; in places it's 180 feet to the crashing white water and the chasm is around 20 feet wide.

A few miles farther the **Reflection Lakes** provide rippling, impressionistic images of Mount Rainier. Finally, you enter ❸ **Paradise**★★, so called by early travelers who thought the landscape so heavenly that no other name would do. The foreground consists of subalpine meadows renowned for their summer wildflowers. Avalanche lilies, red mountainheath, marsh marigolds, magenta painted cup, partridge foot, and many other species thrust their brilliant blossoms into the sunlight

Snowshoeing, Mount Rainier

Northwest Trek Wildlife Park

in a passionate effort to reproduce during the brief summer. Several creeks and dozens of thin, murmuring rivulets flash down the slopes amid clumps of fir, cedar, and hemlock.

Many trails thread through these meadows. **Nisqually Vista Trail**★, an easy, 1.2-mile interpretive loop, swings across the meadows to the rim of the ravine above the snout of **Nisqually Glacier.** The more strenuous, 6-mile **Skyline Trail**★★ ascends along the eastern flank of the glacier up into the alpine, then descends back through idyllic meadows to the **Paradise Inn**★ *(360-569-2275).* Check out (or into) this 1917 lodge. The long, lofty-ceilinged lobby has grand stone fireplaces at either end, a thicket of cedar beams above, and much decorative woodwork, most of which was done one winter by a German carpenter using only an adze. A rustic piano and a towering grandfather clock made by this fine craftsman also grace the lobby. Nearby is the park **Visitor Center**★ *(Daily May-Oct., weekends Nov.-April),* a round building whose displays on the natural and human history of Mount Rainier are reached via a slowly ascending spiral ramp. At the top you emerge into a huge, circular room where floor-to-ceiling windows provide superb views.

From Paradise, 10 winding miles past waterfalls, rock pinnacles, come-hither trails, and dense forest you arrive at **Longmire,** site of a modest park museum, a wilderness information center, a small historic lodge, and an extensive trail network. The short and easy **Trail of the Shadows** includes the mineral springs that motivated James Longmire to develop a health resort in this area in 1884. The road soon leaves the park and becomes Wash. 706. Take this to Wash. 7, detouring to Eatonville, where you pick up Wash. 161 north to ❹ **Northwest Trek Wildlife Park**★ *(360-832-6117 or 800-433-8735. Daily March-Oct., Fri.-Sun. and some holidays rest of year; adm. fee).* Northwest Trek encloses a whopping 435 acres of forest, meadows, and swamps and lets its animals wander freely (except for the wolves, bears, and other predators, which are separately penned). Visitors circulate in trams driven by naturalists. The animals behave pretty much as they would in freedom: Rutting bull elk emit high-pitched squeals and spar with each other; an orange bison calf nurses from its mother; and trumpeter swans sound their bugles.

Galloping Gertie

On July 1, 1940, a soaring, mile-long bridge opened from Tacoma across the narrows to the Kitsap Peninsula. Motorists soon suspected that something was wrong, however. Even moderate winds would make the bridge roadway roll so much that a driver would lose sight of the car ahead of him; hence the nickname "Galloping Gertie." On November 7, 1940, in 42-mile-per-hour winds, Gertie became a bucking bronco and was closed. But Leonard Coatsworth, a local newspaper editor, and his cocker spaniel, Tubby, were stranded on the corkscrewing center span. The frightened dog refused to leave, and Coatsworth finally ran, stumbled, and crawled to safety alone. Soon the bridge began disintegrating piece by piece until the whole ill-fated mass of metal and concrete—and Tubby—collapsed into the water. Don't worry: The current bridge doesn't even trot, let alone gallop.

115

Continue north to Wash. 167 and back to ⑤ **Tacoma**★ *(Visitor Center 206-627-2836 or 800-272-2662).* Start downtown at Tacoma's longtime visual keystone, the immense copper dome of **Union Station** *(1717 Pacific Ave. 206-572-9310. Mon.-Fri.),* built in 1911. Most of this monument to train travel is now a federal courthouse, but the area under the dome holds a fantastic collection of glass art by noted artist Dale Chihuly, a Tacoma native. This exhibit is a branch of the nearby **Tacoma Art Museum** *(Pacific Ave. and 12th St. 206-272-4258. Closed Mon.; adm. fee),* which houses a varied collection in a historic bank building.

But don't leave the area just yet. In 1996, the **Washington State History Museum**★★ *(1911 Pacific Ave. 206-272-3500 or 888-238-4373. Closed Mon. Labor Day–Mem. Day; adm. fee)* moved right next to Union Station, its towering brick archways reflecting the landmark architecture of its venerable neighbor. This is the finest history museum in the Northwest, offering an exceptional depth of information made lively in a multitude of ways. A computer-animated tabletop map shows the geologic evolution of Washington; by pressing buttons, visitors make mountains rise and rivers change course. At "Small Fry Outfitters," kids don pioneer clothing. You can listen to an audio program on southern coast Salish life inside a plank house built by a native craftsman using traditional tools, materials, and methods. The museum also tackles hard and sometimes controversial subjects, such as the nuclear pollution at the Hanford Site and the job discrimination against blacks perpetrated by Boeing in the 1940s.

View Tacoma's vital shipping industry by taking the 11th Street Bridge to the docks and proceeding to the **Port Observation Tower** *(206-383-5841. Call for directions)* beside the Port of Tacoma office . From the tower you can get good looks at several monster cranes as they load and unload ships in this sixth largest of America's container ports.

Just north of downtown, echoes of the past surface in the **Stadium-Seminary Historic District,** anchored by

Tacoma skyline

Stadium High School *(111 North E St.).* Originally designed as a resort hotel, this 1891 exaggeration of a French château bristles with spires and turrets. Nearby is **Wright Park**—the whole park is on the National Register of Historic Places—and its centerpiece, the 1908 **W. W. Seymour Botanical Conservatory** *(316 South G St. 206-591-5330).* This glass-domed Victorian shelters more than 500 species of tropical plants. Across G Street is an often overlooked treasure: the **Karpeles Manuscript Library Museum**★ *(407 South G St. 206-383-2575. Closed Mon.),* one of seven Karpeles museums in the country. Selections from the extensive collection are displayed for nonscholars in two rooms. Typically, one room follows a theme. An exhibit on medical history, for example, showed handwritten documents and letters from Benjamin Franklin, Clara Barton, Louis Pasteur, Florence Nightingale, and many others. The other room offers a potpourri, such as a 17th-century map that shows California as an island.

Tacoma's Union Station

The 700 forested acres of **Point Defiance Park**★★ occupy the peninsula that juts into Puget Sound from northwest Tacoma. The scenic **Five Mile Drive** serves up trails, picnic areas, an understory of rhododendrons, and views of the sound. The park also holds **Fort Nisqually Historic Site** *(206-591-5339. Daily Mem. Day–Labor Day, Wed.-Sun. rest of year; adm. fee),* a reproduction of an 1840s Hudson's Bay Company post, and **Camp 6 Logging Museum** *(206-752-0047. Mid-Jan.–Oct. Wed.-Sun.),* where artifacts and displays detail life in Northwest logging camps from 1880 to 1950.

The park's highlight is the **Point Defiance Zoo & Aquarium**★★ *(206-591-5335. Adm. fee),* which concentrates on the animals of the Pacific Rim. That theme allows great latitude—literally—and includes musk oxen from the high Arctic, tiger quolls from Australia, lemurs from Southeast Asia, and Northwest natives, such as sea otters, puffins, and Dungeness crabs. Explore the humid tropics at the **Discovery Reef Aquarium**★ and descend into an ocean reef. The incredible numbers and variety of sharks are especially engaging. Go to the other ends of the earth to see the excellent exhibits of polar creatures, and hang around for the rude nose-blowing antics of the walruses—sure to delight the kids—and the penguin choir, wherein Magellanic penguins crowd together, raise their preposterous bills to the sky, and squawk and honk in raucous song.

Southwest Corner

● **260 miles** ● **2 to 3 days** ● **Spring through autumn**

The lower Columbia River, the Pacific Ocean, Willapa Bay, Mount St. Helens: These natural wonders anchor this drive through southwestern Washington. However, much along the way bears a human imprint, as the river, the ocean, and the bay have been magnets for settlement for hundreds of years. The route encounters a bucolic island community, two 19th-century forts, a kite museum, and several little towns where oysters are king. As for those natural wonders, they include a refuge for a rare species of deer, miles of inviting sandy beach, an ancient cedar forest, salt marshes teeming with wildlife, and the awesome, post-eruption landscape of Mount St. Helens.

Peel off from I-5 in the Longview/Kelso area and steer west on Wash. 4; you'll soon join the Columbia as the massive river makes its final run to the sea. About 25 miles later lies little ❶ **Cathlamet,** an 1846 river town imbedded in the side of a steep hill overlooking the Columbia. A walkabout will reveal a marina that's home port to a few tug boats, a one-chair barber shop, the 1896 Pioneer Church (its steeple served as a navigational aid to riverboat captains), and the **Wahkiakum County Historical Museum** *(River and Division Sts. 360-795-3954. June-Oct. Tues.-Sun., Nov.-May Thurs.-Sun.; donation),* which holds fishing, logging, and pioneer artifacts. The park behind the museum offers fine views of oil tankers, tugs towing barges heaped with wood chips, and other river traffic.

Drive through town and cross the bridge to 2-by-5-mile **Puget Island★**, where side roads invite exploration. Its people are oriented to the water; even the First Free Church has a dock in back. You'll pass prim white houses, a grange hall, houseboats, dairy farms established long ago by Swiss immigrants, and Norse Hall, which suggests the Scandinavian heritage of many fishermen who settled here. On the far side of the island, a small fee will buy you a 12-minute ride across the river to Oregon on the last lower-Columbia ferry *(360-795-3301)*, which has been running since 1925. The tiny boat can hold a dozen or so cars.

A mile past Cathlamet lies the **Julia Butler Hansen National Wildlife Refuge★** *(Wash. 4. 360-795-3915)*, a 4,400-acre riverside spread set aside to protect endangered Columbian white-tailed deer. Flooding in 1996-97 decimated the deer population in this lush preserve of woods, meadows, and marsh that is home to beavers, pileated woodpeckers, Roosevelt elk, river otters, tundra swans, coyotes, bald eagles, and more. Spot wildlife from the road or visit the wildlife viewing site a mile beyond the Steamboat Slough Road entrance.

Continue to the junction of Wash. 4 and 401. Take Wash. 401

Covered bridge, Grays River near Astoria-Megler Bridge

south 12 miles to the **Astoria-Megler Bridge,** spanning the mouth of the Columbia between Washington and Oregon. Pick up US 101 as it comes over the bridge and

Cape Disappointment Lighthouse, near Ilwaco

go west to **Fort Columbia State Park** *(360-777-8221 or 360-642-3078. Visitor Center and museum May-Sept. Wed.-Sun., grounds April-Sept.)*. This artillery post was built in the 1890s to help defend the entrance to the Columbia. As you wander amid the restored gun emplacements, appreciate the commanding views of the river's mouth selected by the fort's designers. The Visitor Center and museum provide an introduction to the lives of the area's pioneers, Chinook Indians, and soldiers. Take the time to read some of the old documents on display, from touching love letters to the cooking advice offered in an 1883 Army cook's manual: "Remember that beans, badly boiled, kill more than bullets...."

More exhibits await just up US 101 in ❷ **Ilwaco** *(Visitor Center 360-642-2400 or 800-451-2542)* at the **Ilwaco Heritage Museum**★ *(115 S.E. Lake St. 360-642-3446. Closed Sun. Oct.-April; adm. fee)*. Start at the excellent displays on the Chinook, the tribe that controlled the mouth of the Columbia and whose jargon served as the region's trade language. Tragically, their position exposed the Chinook to many European traders and the diseases they carried; by the 1830s some 90 percent of the tribal members had died, and by 1890 an anthropologist could find only two fluent speakers of Chinook alive. A room devoted to the Columbia estuary features a 12-by-8-foot working model in which water shows the tidal action and its effects on the environment. Another exhibit focuses on Gerard d'Aboville's 134-day solo crossing of the Pacific from Japan to Ilwaco in 1991—he *rowed*.

From Ilwaco drive 3 miles south to **Fort Canby State Park** *(360-642-3078)*. An Army base from 1864 to 1957, the site still has bunkers and batteries from its military days, but today its main allures are the peaceful pursuits of beachcombing, fishing, hiking, and visiting the 1898 **North Head Lighthouse** *(Tours daily in summer and by appt.)*. High on a bluff at the park's south end sits the **Lewis and Clark Interpretive Center**★ *(360-642-3029. Donation)*, not far from where the intrepid explorers first encountered the Pacific. Ramps lead along a time line of paintings, photos, and artifacts that take visitors with Meriwether Lewis and William Clark from Illinois to the mouth of the Columbia. You'll learn that Thomas Jefferson, who dispatched Lewis and Clark during his presidency, deceived rival foreign powers by labeling the expedition a "literary pursuit." Read a journal account of western science's first encounter with prairie dogs; the explorers poured five barrels of water down a hole in a futile attempt to flush one out. At the top of the building there's a high-windowed viewing room with great vistas of the Columbia's mouth and untold square miles of ocean and coast. Within walking distance stands the 1856 **Cape Disappointment Lighthouse** *(No tours)*, which visitors can also reach via a trail from the parking lot of the Interpretive Center.

Head north on US 101 for 2 miles to Seaview, where you can explore the **Long Beach Peninsula**★ by continuing north along the coast on Wash. 103. First you'll hit the tourist town of **Long Beach** *(Visitor Center 360-642-2400 or 800-451-2542)*. Given the abundance of gift shops, restaurants, and motels, it comes as a surprise that the boardwalk is a half-mile, elevated wooden walkway with interpretive signs that leads above the dune grass of a semiwild beach. In fact, development has been kept off the beach on much of the peninsula. Back on the main drag, visitors can delve into this town's mania for kites by stopping at the **World Kite Museum and Hall of Fame** *(3rd St. N. and Pacific Hwy. 360-642-4020. Daily June-Aug., Fri.-Mon. Sept.-Oct., Sat.-Sun. Nov.-May; adm. fee)*.

About 10 miles north of Long Beach, Wash. 103 leaves the ocean and cuts across the narrow peninsula to the turn-of-the-century oyster port of **Nahcotta**★ on beautiful **Willapa Bay.** Amble down past 25-foot-high mountains of oyster shells to the docks and learn about the ecology of this oyster-friendly estuary and its 150-year history of oystering at the **Willapa Bay Interpretive Center** *(On the dock. 360-665-4547. Mem. Day–mid-Oct. Fri.-Sun.; donation)*.

Graveyard of the Pacific

Over the years, the treacherous waters where the Columbia River meets the Pacific Ocean have claimed nearly 2,000 vessels. Sailors must be especially alert when crossing the bar—the shoal of sand and gravel at the mouth of the river. Due to the exceptional danger posed by the area, the Life Saving Service (ancestor of the U.S. Coast Guard) established a station on Cape Disappointment in 1873. Present-day visitors to the Lewis and Clark Interpretive Center pass by the entrance to a major Coast Guard station and the U.S. Coast Guard Motor Lifeboat School, where the students' training includes surf drills and other such hair-raising maneuvers. Training exercises can sometimes be seen from the lighthouse.

Oysterville sign

Stealing the County Seat

On the wintry Sunday of February 5, 1893, around 85 men from South Bend, Washington, slipped across Willapa Bay in two steamers to the little town of Oysterville, then the Pacific County seat. They expected all the Oystervillians to be in church, but a lone figure holding a shotgun blocked their way on the wharf. After a brief parlay with the gunman, he let them pass—on the condition that they first buy a round of drinks in the saloon he owned. Thus refreshed, the mob continued to the county courthouse, where a tailor named John Hudson kicked in the door. The men took some of the county records and furniture back to South Bend and proclaimed their town the county seat, a status South Bend has enjoyed ever since.

The present state of oystering can be observed by strolling the dock, which overlooks some of the oyster beds. Oyster boats bob in the marina and thousands of net sacks packed with oyster shells are piled around the busy seafood canneries. Stop at their retail outlets and pick up some clams, crabs (in season), or a bucket of fresh oysters. It is said that this incredibly productive bay produces about one out of every six oysters eaten in the United States.

Three miles north lies the quaint, tiny town of **Oysterville★**. Founded in 1854, it essentially consists of a few streets lined by well-kept 19th-century houses, a few compatible newer houses, a historic one-room schoolhouse, an exquisite little park, and an 1892 church topped by a tall, slender steeple. Take a leisurely walk through town and appreciate the details, such as antique roses in the many fine gardens and original hand-carved pickets in some of the white picket fences.

From Oysterville, take Stackpole Road north 3 miles to ❸ **Leadbetter Point State Park** *(360-642-3078)* and the Leadbetter Unit of the **Willapa National Wildlife Refuge★** *(Call state park)*, which between them occupy the tip of the Long Beach Peninsula. Trails wind through a varied landscape of conifer forest, sandy beach, marsh, and mudflat. Wildlife abounds; in certain seasons you can observe thousands of Canada geese, warblers, and various shorebirds.

Back on US 101 heading northeast, you will pass other units of the national wildlife refuge as you skirt the eastern shore of Willapa Bay. After 40 scenic miles, just as the highway leaves the bay for good, comes ❹ **South Bend** *(Chamber of Commerce 360-875-5231)*, which bills itself as the Oyster Capital of the World (see sidebar this page). Indeed, from the little bayfront park at the city's center you can see oysters rattling up a conveyor belt from the dock to the Coast Seafoods Company. Across the highway from the park is the **Pacific County Museum** *(1008 W. Robert Bush Dr. 360-875-5224)*, whose displays on logging, fishing, and railroads reveal that there's more to the county than oysters. Like a king on his throne, the surprisingly lavish 1910 **Pacific County Courthouse** *(Call Chamber of Commerce to arrange tours)* sits atop Quality Hill above downtown. Note the gorgeous art glass dome above the rotunda and the display of historical photos, including some of the Raymond flood of 1933.

Drive east on US 101 toward neighboring Raymond, then southeast on Wash. 6 back to I-5. As you move south back to Longview/Kelso to complete the loop, get off at

Castle Rock for a drive that has held special significance since May 18, 1980, the day Mount St. Helens erupted.

North side of Mount St. Helens

To learn about the eruption and its aftermath, drive east on Wash. 504 to **⑤ Mount St. Helens National Volcanic Monument**★ ★ *(Headquarters 360-274-3900. Adm. fee)*. Motorists won't reach the edge of the monument for 37 miles, but a variety of facilities along the road rate a stop, beginning with the **Mount St. Helens Visitor Center** *(360-247-2100)* at **Silver Lake**★ ★, 5 miles from Castle Rock. Under its soaring roof you can enjoy videos of the eruption, a seismograph that allows you to "make a quake" by jumping up and down, a map tracing the extent of the ash fall (as far as Montana), and a walk-through model of the mountain's insides that shows how the earth's forces came together to cause the eruption.

Mount St. Helens Visitor Center

As you continue up Wash. 504, also known as the Spirit Lake Memorial Highway, you will encounter some kind of volcano-related site every few miles. **Hoffstadt Bluffs**

Visitor Center *(360-274-7750)*, 22 miles past the Silver Lake Visitor Center, provides the first full view of Mount St. Helens. Its gallery and gift shop feature much gray pottery and sculpture-items fashioned from the ash that blanketed the region after the 1980 eruption.

Six miles beyond, the **Forest Learning Center**★ *(360-414-3439. Mid-May–Oct.)* features extensive exhibits on how the center's main sponsor, timber giant Weyerhaeuser, reforested its holdings that were devastated by the volcanic blast and the ensuing mud flows. From a vantage point outside the center, visitors often can spot a large elk herd.

In this vicinity, travelers enter the part of the blast zone where all the trees were blown down. It's an eerie experience to drive through this scalped landscape. Four miles from the Forest Learning Center you cross into the monument proper, and 6 miles later awaits the last center, the **Coldwater Ridge Visitor Center**★ ★ *(360-274-2131)*. From its observation decks, a mere 7 miles from the crater, you can really sense the awesome force that was unleashed on that May day in 1980. As you stare into the huge gouge on the north face of the volcano, you can imagine the top 1,300 feet of the mountain suddenly collapsing in the biggest landslide ever recorded. The enormous deposits of now-hardened mud and ash in the valley below Coldwater Ridge are reminders of that 15-mile-long tide of rock, soil, ice, and trees, an explosion heard in parts of Canada 700 miles away.

Knowing the devastating force of the eruption, many visitors expect to find an utterly barren moonscape, but that's far from the case. Excellent displays and programs at the Coldwater Ridge Visitor Center explain how life is returning to the blast zone. For example, birds and bugs flew in before the ash had even settled. Lupine and fireweed grew out of the ash within a couple of months. Within five years elk and deer numbers had returned to normal. Take the time to wander the **Winds of Change Interpretive Trail** *(Limited access in winter)* as it traverses through a sliver of the blast zone so you can see the process of renewal in action. Ten miles from the center is the **Johnson Ridge Observatory** *(360-274-2140. May-Oct.)*. From here, you can gaze directly across the valley into the crater, a mere 5 miles away.

Return down Wash. 504 to I-5. If you thirst for more of Mount St. Helens, you can drive around the monument and explore it from the east and south sides, as well. Those who have had enough can go south on the interstate and be back in Longview/Kelso in ten minutes.

Grand Gorge

● 185 miles ● 2 to 3 days ● Spring through autumn

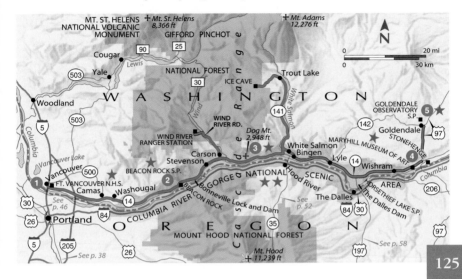

Great prehistoric lava flows hardened into the basalt that formed the raw material for the Columbia River Gorge. Eons later, great floods of water from melting ice caps scoured channels within the basalt into the deep corridor of waterfalls, cliffs, and side canyons that visitors admire today. This drive tours the Washington side of the gorge, starting from the historic city of Vancouver. The route goes east through small towns and flagrantly scenic landscapes, passing dams, fish hatcheries, an eccentric art museum, and the Columbia River Gorge. The drive ends at an observatory amid rolling, high-desert hills.

❶ **Vancouver** *(Chamber of Commerce 360-694-2588 or 800-377-7084)* is the oldest city in Washington, so it's no surprise that history is its strong suit. Many fine old buildings remain downtown, including **St. James Catholic Church** *(218 W. 12th St. 360-693-3052)*, an 1885 Victorian Gothic Revival-style brick edifice, and **Covington House** *(4201 Main St. 360-695-6750. June-Aug. Tues. and Thurs.)*, a log house dating from 1848. Going even farther back in time is **Fort Vancouver National Historic Site** ★ *(1501 Evergreen Blvd. 360-696-7655. Adm. fee May-Sept.)*, where Hudson's Bay Company, the famed

Canon, Fort Vancouver National Historic Site

British concern, set up a major trading post in the 1820s. By 1845—the era depicted in this authentic re-creation—the fort was the hub of the Northwest. Park interpreters show visitors around the large complex, which includes a trade shop, a bastion, a blacksmith's shop, and the chief factor's elegant residence.

Walkway above the Columbia River Gorge, Beacon Rock State Park

Nearby on the **Vancouver National Historic Reserve**, is **Officers' Row** *(360-693-3103. Call for hours)*, a remnant of the U.S. Army complex started around 1850 to fortify America's claim to this area. Visitors can tour the **Gen. George C. Marshall House** *(1301 Officers' Row. 360-693-3101)*, a lovely Queen Anne Victorian, and the **U.S. Grant House** *(1101 Officers' Row. 360-694-5252. Tues.-Sat.)*, the row's earliest residence. Walk or drive by the other 19 officers' houses, built between 1850 and 1906. Late in 1997, the **Gen. O.O. Howard House** *(750 Anderson Rd.)* will open as an Interpretive Center and as the Visitor Center for all the attractions on the reserve, including the **Pearson Air Museum** in the new **Jack Murdock Aviation Center** *(360-694-7026. Call for hours; adm. fee)*. Planes, artifacts, and photos evoke the rich and entertaining history of U.S. aviation from 1905 to 1945.

Another new attraction on this dynamic reserve is the **Water Resources Education Center**★ *(360-696-8478. Closed Sun.)*. Appropriately set beside a 40-acre wetland and the Columbia River, the center uses art, videos, computers, hands-on exhibits, and other methods to explain water stewardship, with an emphasis on the Columbia Basin.

About a dozen miles east on Wash. 14 the route enters the **Columbia River Gorge National Scenic Area**★★ *(Headquarters in Hood River, Oregon. 541-386-2333)*, which encompasses most of the drive. With the nation's second largest river on the right and dark, brooding basalt cliffs on the left, the road eases along the narrow strip of flat land for about 20 miles to ❷ **Beacon Rock State Park**★ *(Wash. 14. 509-427-8265. April-Oct.)*. Steps—many, many steps—allow people to labor to the top of this 848-foot volcanic plug. The views of the

Columbia and surrounding wilderness merit the effort.

Five miles east lies another monumental structure, this one made by humans. **Bonneville Lock and Dam** *(541-374-8820)* was completed in 1937, with a second powerhouse added in 1982 (see sidebar p. 53). From the Washington side of the river, travelers can stop in at the second powerhouse, which features a Visitor Center, a fish ladder, underwater fish-viewing windows, and a self-guided tour that goes inside part of a generator.

In **Stevenson** *(Chamber of Commerce 509-427-8911 or 800-989-9178),* visit the **Columbia Gorge Interpretive Center**★ *(990 S.W. Rock Creek Dr. 509-427-8211. Adm. fee).* This facility feels like the gorge, from the waterfall to the soaring 40-foot ceiling to the rock walls fabricated from molds of the gorge's cliffs. The exhibits start with petroglyphs and information about the creation myths of the area's first peoples. Next come collections of Indian artifacts, including a noteworthy display of baskets and bead necklaces. Extensive exhibits tell of the fur traders and pioneers; imagine wearing the full-length bear coat. A centerpiece is the 37-foot-tall fish wheel; these contraptions decimated the Columbia's salmon populations between 1880 and the 1920s. The natural history of the gorge also is covered, starting with a rumbling, flashing theater presentation on the formation of the gorge.

127

A short walk up the hill stands **Skamania Lodge** *(1131 S.W. Skamania Lodge Way. 509-427-7700 or 800-221-7117),* a resort that is woodsy yet polished. The pretty dining room looks out over the gorge, artwork derived from Columbia River petroglyphs decorates the walls, and a U.S. Forest Service information office *(509-427-2528)* is in the lobby.

Windsurfing, Columbia River

Just up Wash. 14 is Stevenson proper, whose pleasant little downtown offers a couple of decent art galleries, cafés, and a waterfront park. Five miles beyond, in the town of Carson, turn north on Wind River Road. Following the river into the **Wind River Valley**★, this road provides access to hiking, backpacking, fishing, and camping in a grand expanse of Cascades backcountry. About 9 miles along, stop in at the **Wind River Ranger**

Station *(509-427-3200. Permit required for some usages).*
Here helpful rangers can provide information about
Lower Falls Creek Trail, an easy 2-mile hike through fine
forest to the misty base of a 180-foot waterfall. Or ask
about **Grassy Knoll Trail,** a longer, steeper path that in
season rewards hikers with opulent wildflower meadows
and loads of huckleberries.

Blessed though it is with fine trails, the Wind River
Valley hardly has a monopoly on them. Back on Wash. 14,
continue east about 9 miles from Stevenson and you'll
come to one of the best hikes in the gorge, the ❸ **Dog
Mountain Trail**★. The three routes to the top (you can
choose among steep, steeper, and oh-my-aching-legs)
begin in appealing forest, but Dog Mountain's fame stems
from the hundreds of acres of meadows around the
summit. Sloping at angles just short of dangerous, in mid-
May these meadows overflow with balsam root, penste-
mon, phlox, lupine, and other brilliant wildflowers. While
basking amid the blossoms, rubber-legged hikers also can
relish sweeping views of the gorge and the Cascades.

Just after Wash. 14 crosses the **White Salmon River,**
turn left on Wash. 141A and head north up the road cling-
ing to the east bank. Soon the road joins Wash. 141 and
proceeds to the stretch of the White Salmon that has been
designated a national scenic river. Local outfitters offer rafting trips down this beautiful reach. Continue up Wash. 141
through vast pear orchards and forest to the community of
Trout Lake and the **Mount Adams Ranger District** *(Ranger
Station 509-395-3400. Access limited in winter. Permit required
for some usages).* Rangers can steer you to nearby trails,
wilderness areas, huckleberry fields, lakes, lava beds, and
to **Ice Cave.** On a hot summer day, it's refreshing to
descend the wooden stairway into this natural ice box.
Walk a few feet into the ancient lava tube (beware of slippery ice) and shine a flashlight on the ice formations;
they're reminiscent of the stalactites, stalagmites, columns,
curtains, and other shapes one sees in limestone caverns.
Adventurers wishing to explore the 650-foot-long cave further should consult with rangers about safety concerns.

As you continue east on Wash. 14, watch the deep,
forested gorge give way to grassy hills and dramatic
basalt-peppered plateaus. About 20 miles along, turn
right down to the river at **Horsethief Lake State Park**
(509-767-1159. Nov.-March). It's mildly popular for fishing,
boating, and picnicking, but it's famous for the abundant
petroglyphs on the hillside, which was at various times
inhabited by several local Native American peoples. The

Stonehenge

Maryhill Museum of Art
was not the only result of
Sam Hill's potent blend of
wealth, imagination, and
idiosyncrasy. In 1907 he
bought 7,000 acres just
east of Maryhill with the
intent of founding a
Quaker agricultural
utopia. The Quaker
community fell through, but
Hill, an ardent pacifist,
later built a full-scale recreation of Stonehenge on
part of the site. Hill had
heard that the ancient
neolithic ruins in England
had been the site of human
sacrifice (a theory now dis-
credited), so he thought
Stonehenge a fitting post-
World War I reminder that
"humanity is still being sac-
rificed to the god of war."
Hill's crypt sits on the edge
of the bluff a hundred feet
from Stonehenge.

petroglyphs are accessible only via ranger-led tours *(Fri. and Sat. a.m., call ahead)*.

As you're sailing down Wash. 14, passing through sparsely populated ranch lands, you'll see what seems to be a mirage on the bluff above the river. That would be the ❹ **Maryhill Museum of Art**★ *(509-773-3733. Mid-March–mid-Nov.; adm. fee)*. Designed in the fashion of a château, this enormous mansion was originally built in the 1910s as the home of Sam Hill, a wealthy and eccentric Seattle businessman (see sidebar p. 128). The collection belies Maryhill's remoteness. It includes a renowned group of French fashion mannequins, more than a hundred exquisite and curious antique chess sets, and an internationally recognized collection of sculpture and drawings by Auguste Rodin.

Just east of Maryhill, take US 97 north to **Goldendale**

Fourth of July in Goldendale

(Chamber of Commerce 509-773-3400). Foremost among the small farm town's historic buildings is the elegant **Presby Mansion** *(Broadway and Grant Sts. 509-773-4303. April-Oct.; adm. fee)*, which also holds the **Klickitat County Historical Society Museum.** The 20 rooms contain all sorts of items, from a bear trap big enough to catch Godzilla to an attic full of old ranching gear to a whole bunch of coffee grinders.

Complete the drive by going out of this world at ❺ **Goldendale Observatory State Park**★ *(1602 Observatory Dr. 509-773-3141. April-Sept. Wed.-Sun., Oct.-March Sat.-Sun. and by appt.)*. Visitors can scan the night sky with one of the largest public-use telescopes in the nation, the kind usually reserved for astronomers. A half dozen other substantial telescopes and interpretive programs make the observatory heaven for stargazers. Look up and enjoy.

Into the Interior★

● 670 miles ● 4 to 5 days ● Summer ● Denali Highway is impassable from roughly mid-October to mid-May.

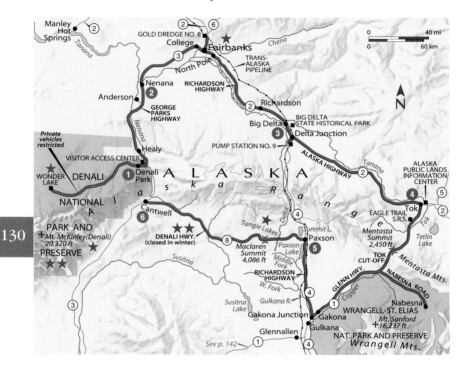

Junior Rangers, Denali National Park

The interior is Alaska's frontier. Most Alaskans have settled on the southern coast, a more lenient landscape. The interior is the land of short trees and long winters. The majority of Alaska's great heartland only can be reached by bush plane, if it can be reached at all, but this drive allows motorists to sample this harsh yet striking region. The loop includes inland Alaska's only city, outstanding wildlife-watching, some colorful backcountry lodges, an exceptional museum, river-rafting opportunities, the country's largest national park, Alaska's most popular national park, and wide, wide open spaces.

The harmonious howls of a wolf pack drift on the wind. A natural bonsai garden hugs the tundra in obeisance to ruthless winters. Roly-poly marmots wrestle and chase through their rocky meadows. The "Mountain," lord of the land, hulks above everything. There are many facets to the drive's starting point,

1 **Denali National Park and Preserve** ★ ★ *(907-683-2294. Visitor facilities mid-May–mid-Sept.; adm. fee).* The park's diversity stems partly from its size; at more than 6 million acres it's larger than Massachusetts.

Denali is a wilderness, and the park has established several measures to keep it that way despite the hundreds of thousands of visitors who descend here each summer. All traffic, established trails, lodging (with a few minor exceptions), and commercial development are restricted to the

Buses entering Denali National Park and Preserve

area near the entrance. Visitors can't go beyond Milepost 14.8 on the park road unless they're on a bicycle, on foot, or on a shuttle or tour bus. Reservations for campsites *(fee)* and seats on the shuttle buses *(fee)* are allocated by the **Visitor Access Center** *(907-272-7275 or 800-622-7275. Call ahead).*

Sled dog demonstrations, naturalist walks, a variety of hiking trails, and many other diversions are also available in the entrance area. By all means enjoy these activities, but by no means stop there. These are the opening acts; the headliner waits beyond Mile 15. Get on the bus and go west; if you have the stamina for the 12-hour journey, travel all 85 miles to **Wonder Lake** ★ —and back.

The trip starts in taiga, the skimpy forest of spruce peppered with aspen, birch, alder, and poplar. The road soon climbs above 2,700 feet, timberline at this far northern latitude, and travelers emerge into the treeless world of the tundra. The lack of trees creates dizzying views of rolling hills, great braided rivers, and shark-tooth mountains. It makes for clear views of the abundant wildlife, too. The use of buses also enhances animal-watching; rather than scaring animals, the buses serve as blinds that provide close-up looks at animals behaving naturally. A grizzly may dig out an Arctic ground squirrel 100 feet from your

Grizzly, Denali National Park

Wildflowers, Denali National Park

132

window. A band of caribou may gallop up a nearby ridge, their improbable antlers etching a striking silhouette. Moose may dip their faces into ponds to graze on underwater vegetation.

One way of experiencing Denali surpasses even those bus rides—getting off the bus. Virtually anytime during the ride on park shuttle buses (although not the private tour buses), passengers can step out into raw nature. (Be sure to pick up backcountry tips at the Visitor Center beforehand.) When the bus disappears around the bend, you'll be left standing in a realm that hasn't changed much in thousands of years. Walk a way into the tundra, feel the cushion of plants beneath your feet, and breathe that pure air. Listen to that thrumming quiet—perhaps you'll hear the call of the wild. When you're ready to return to the present, flag down a passing bus.

Whether you're on the bus or on your own, keep an

Mount McKinley, also known as Denali, and Wonder Lake

eye out for "The High One," Denali itself, also known as **Mount McKinley**★. Frequent clouds often obscure the mountain, and even when the park's lower elevations are clear and sunny, clouds may shroud the mountain. But keep looking, for if it ever appears you'll almost feel as if McKinley's leaning over you, even though it is at least 20 miles away from roadside viewpoints. It's the biggest vertical rise in the world: 18,000 feet from the flats near the base to the 20,320-foot summit.

Leaving Denali, head north on the George Parks Highway lined with lodges, rafting outfits, souvenir shops, and other services aimed at park visitors. Near **Healy** you may glimpse an enormous piece of machinery digging for coal seams at the **Usibelli Coal Mine;** it's a walking dragline and it weighs 4,276,000 pounds. The highway plays tag with the **Nenana River** for about 55 miles until they both reach the confluence with the **Tanana River.** This major river crossroads spawned the town of ❷ **Nenana** *(Visitor Center, George Parks Hwy. and A St. 907-832-9953. Mem. Day–Labor Day),* which boomed as a base for the Alaskan Railroad. The site at which President Warren G. Harding drove the golden spike in 1923 lies just across the Tanana from

Nenana Ice Classic

Exactly when the ice-bound Tanana River at Nenana will break up has been the subject of wagering since 1917. Each winter Nenanians set up a big tripod on the frozen river and run a line from the tripod to a clock in a building on shore. When the ice breaks up in April or May the tripod falls and stops the clock, determining the winning time. Back in 1917 a few guys in Nenana bet on break-up and the prize was $800. Today tens of thousands of Alaskans wager hundreds of thousands of dollars on the Nenana Ice Classic; total prize money in 1996 was about $300,000.

133

downtown. The railroad's saga is told at the historic 1923 depot, now the **Alaska Railroad Museum** *(Front and A Sts. 907-832-9953. Mem. Day–Labor Day).*

Nenana's

Native graphic, near Anderson

past as a river port surfaces as soon as you stop by the Visitor Center; behind it sits the *Taku Chief,* an old tug that used to push barges on the Tanana. For a look at the present tugs and barges, visit the docks. During the summer, after the ice on the rivers has broken up, many tons of freight move between Nenana and remote villages along the Tanana and Yukon Rivers.

Travelers 70 years ago might have taken a stern-wheeler from Nenana, but motorists can now continue on the highway as it turns east along the Tanana and drive the 50 miles into **Fairbanks** ★ *(Visitor Center 907-456-5774 or 800-327-5774).* This city of some 33,000 lies in the heart of the Alaskan interior and serves as its hub. Not bad for a place that was founded by accident.

In 1901 a fortune hunter and con man named E.T. Barnette was heading up the Tanana River on a stern-wheeler, bound for Tanana Crossing, the midway point on the Valdez-Eagle Trail. He intended to set up a trading post to take advantage of the travelers heading to and from the goldfields. But as the boat started up the Chena River the water got too shallow and the river boat captain dumped the protesting Barnette and all his trade goods on the river bank. Having no choice, he went ahead and set up a trading post in the middle of nowhere, his prospects for customers dim.

Golden Heart Park, Fairbanks

But Barnette got lucky—a year later gold was discovered 12 miles away. Barnette did some fast talking to draw miners and regional government offices to his town. He quickly grew rich, although some of his previous dealings —grand larceny, for one—eventually caught up with him and he was driven from town in disgrace.

One facet of Fairbanks's gold-mining history comes to life at **Gold Dredge Number 8** *(Mile 9, 1755 Old Steese Hwy.*

907-457-6058. *Mem. Day–Labor Day; adm. fee).* One of a small fleet of big dredges that extracted gold from creek beds around Fairbanks, the five-story, 250-foot-long Number 8 operated from 1928 to 1959. You can tour the dredge, look through an accompanying museum, and even pan for gold.

The gold rush and other Alaskan historical eras are presented in all sorts of ways at **Alaskaland** *(Airport Way and Peger Rd. 907-459-1087. Different sections have different schedules, but everything is open in summer, call for schedule; fee for some attractions).* It's a theme park, but amid the clutter are numerous worthy sites. Besides, in summer Fairbanks does get hot enough for an ice-cream cone. Alaskaland houses several museums. One, the **Alaska Native Village Museum,** examines the Athapaskan culture through artifacts, arts and crafts, and native performances. The **Pioneer Museum** covers the early days of settlement, particularly the gold stampedes, first to the Klondike and then to Fairbanks. Visitors can tour the **S.S. *Nenana,*** a grand old wooden stern-wheeler that plied the Yukon River from 1935 to 1957. To understand the time and place in which the ship operated, study the 340-foot-long diorama (the *Nenana* is a huge ship) that depicts a stretch of the Yukon in painstaking detail, complete with settlements and native villages. A few miles away, sample an active river boat; the stern-wheeler ***Discovery III*** *(1975 Discovery Dr. 907-479-6673. Mid-May–mid-Sept.; fare)* takes passengers on a four-hour cruise on the Chena and Tanana Rivers, stopping for presentations on dog sledding and native culture.

Discovery III, along the Chena River

Alaskan history and just about every other facet of the state is covered at the **University of Alaska Museum**★ *(907 Yukon Dr. 907-474-7505. Adm. fee).* Visitors are greeted by a nearly 9-foot-tall, 1,250-pound grizzly bear—stuffed, fortunately. The bear introduces the museum's noteworthy natural history collection, one of the museum's two main strengths. It's fun simply to gawk at the 10-foot-long mammoth tusks, the bowhead whale skull, and the other items. But you can learn surprising things if you look closely and read the notes. For example, notice the claws on the ringed seal's front flippers and find out that it used them for maintaining breathing holes in the ice.

A discovery that surprised even the scientists is presented in the Boulder Patch exhibit: In the frigid Beaufort Sea, high above the Arctic Circle, encased in ice during the long winters, the bottom of the sea is virtually lifeless—except in the Boulder Patch. Here an underwater garden of kelp, sea anemones, sea stars, clams, and hundreds of other plant and animal species somehow survive, even prosper.

Superb exhibits on Alaska's natives portray the museum's other main strength. Delicate, 2,000-year-old Eskimo ivory carvings; modern Athapascan masks, such as one elegant creation of gleaming black walnut fringed with duck and ptarmigan feathers; a finely detailed Tlingit totem pole tells the story of Raven saving his nephews from the great flood; a video shows traditional Eskimos in small boats using harpoons to hunt whales: The collection is large and varied. The museum also tackles controversial native issues; one extensive exhibit recalls the devastating internment of Alaskan Aleuts by the United States government during World War II.

On campus just down the hill from the museum sprouts the **Georgeson Botanical Garden** *(W. Tanana Dr. 907-474-7200. May-Sept.; fee for guided tour Fri. p.m.).* This 5-acre spread of flowers, fruits, trees, and herbs is the hemisphere's northernmost botanical garden. A guided tour points out how plants cope with the fierce winters of interior Alaska. After mid-July, visitors can marvel at some of the state's fabled giant vegetables.

If you saw any caribou in Denali National Park and Preserve, chances are they were on a ridge or in some other windy location. The reason is simple; after caribou shed much of their hair in the summer, they can lose as much as a pint of blood a day to mosquitoes if they don't find the sanctuary of a stiff breeze. Such fun tidbits of knowledge, plus an introduction to sophisticated ecological concepts, are presented at the university's **Large Animal Research Station (LARS)** ★ *(Yankovich Rd., 1.7 miles off Ballaine Rd. 907-474-7207. Guided tours Tues., Thurs., and Sat. June–Aug., Sat. only in Sept.; viewing platforms open year-round; fee for tour).* LARS scientists study the ways in which musk oxen, caribou, and reindeer have adapted to the rigors of Arctic life. It's informative just to be so close (within a few feet) to these large Arctic ungulates. For example, when you're near walking caribou you can hear their feet

Big Delta State Historical Park

popping like so many knuckles cracking. But to really enrich
the experience join one of the scientist-led tours; they elaborate greatly on what you see and hear. Those caribou feet,
for instance, are not arthritic. The popping comes from the
elastic energy stored in their ligaments and tendons, which
helps conserve energy during their long migrations. And in
deep snow it's hard to keep watch while grazing, so caribou
listen for that popping to know when the herd is stirring.

To see a microcosm of wild interior Alaska without
leaving the Fairbanks city limits, head over to **Creamers
Field Migratory Waterfowl Refuge**★ *(1300 College Rd.
907-459-7307. Guided tours summer only).* Watching the
squabbling flocks of migratory birds that frequent the fields
of this more than 1,600-acre refuge is enjoyable, but best
are the easy and exceedingly pleasant nature trails that slip
through the seasonal wetlands and boreal forest. Bring one
of the excellent trail guides, which are keyed to numbered
stops along the trail. In just the right amount of detail,
these guides provide a mix of identification tips for plants
and animals, natural history facts, and discussion of ecological processes. While you're watching for waterfowl,
snowshoe hares, wood frogs, and moose, you can learn
about the role of fire in the boreal forest and the signs that
distinguish willow nibbled by hares from that grazed by
moose. As you wander through the various habitats, bear
in mind that this is the way much of interior Alaska looks.

Continue the loop by taking the Richardson Highway
southeast, tracking the mighty Tanana River, whose multi-
channel bed at times measures more than a mile across.
About 90 miles later, in the small farm town of ❸ **Big
Delta,** take in an impressive view of the Trans-Alaska
Pipeline as it crosses the Tanana. Just across the river, in
Big Delta State Historical Park, you'll find **Rika's Roadhouse** *(907-895-4201),* built in 1910 as one of the series of
roadhouses serving travelers between Valdez and the goldfields around Fairbanks. Nicely renovated in 1986, it now
serves as a gift shop. The grounds include a barnyard
full of animals, the old telegraph station, and a small but
well-stocked historical museum in a sod-roofed log cabin.
Note the monstrous bear trap and the wolf mittens.

Ensconced in the woods a few miles from nearby
Delta Junction is the **Alaska Homestead and Historical
Museum** *(S on Dorshorst Rd. at Mile 141.5 Alaska Hwy. 907-
895-4431. June-Aug.; adm. fee).* Tours of this sprawling old
homestead take in salmon-drying racks, a sled dog team,
antique farm equipment, and an operating sawmill. Take
a jaunt some 7 miles south of Delta Junction on the

137

Into the Interior

Richardson Highway, where travelers can tour the oil pipeline's **Pump Station Number 9** *(907-869-3270. Summer).*

As you proceed southeast on Alas. 2, you're driving on a storied piece of Alaskan history: the **Alaska Highway.** After Pearl Harbor was bombed, the U.S. military feared that Japan would invade Alaska—which did occur in June 1942, when Japanese troops landed in the Aleutian Islands. Knowing military operations in Alaska would require an overland link between Alaska and the lower 48 states, in early 1942 the government sent soldiers and civilians to begin construction of a 1,422-mile highway between Delta Junction and Dawson Creek, British Columbia. It was a daunting mission. The ground was so soggy in places that tractors got hopelessly mired and the road had to be built right over them. Despite such hardships, thousands of workers labored feverishly and completed the vital link by November of that year. So before you start cursing this highway's potholes, remember how tough it was to build.

A little more than 100 miles through this big-sky country brings you to ❹ **Tok,** a tenuous beachhead in the interior wilderness. Spruce forests crowd against developed lots and about a minute's drive in any direction takes you out of town. Start at Tok's comely new **Mainstreet Visitor Center** *(Junction of Alaska Hwy. and Tok Cutoff. 907-883-5775 or 907-883-5887 off-season. May-Sept.),* where locals give free, public talks on dog mushing (Tok is a dog sledding hotbed), subsistence living, and other fitting topics. The center also houses numerous natural history exhibits, most notably the building's centerpiece —a taxidermy tableau of two wolves chasing a Dall's sheep; the sense of motion makes you want to leap from their path.

For more natural history knowledge, stroll across the room to the **Alaska Public Lands Information Center** *(907-883-5666. Closed weekends Mid-Sept.–mid-May),* where you can learn about salmon, grizzlies, lynx, and find out why locals prefer wolverine fur for the hoods and trim on their parkas (frost doesn't accumulate on wolverine guard hairs). There's also a fine exhibit on the Great Tok Fire (see sidebar p. 139), including an incredible photo of local Joe Quinn standing on his roof holding a hose when flames are within 100 feet of his house. If you feel like laughing, albeit bitterly, check out the presentation on what people hate most about Alaska, such as mosquitoes and those ankle-breaking tussocks.

Trans-Alaska Pipeline

Along the Denali Highway between Paxon and Cantwell

To continue the loop, turn south on Alas. 1, also known as the Tok Cut-off. For lovely campgrounds and pleasant hiking trails, visit **Eagle Trail State Recreation Site** *(907-451-2695)* about 16 miles out of Tok. The mile-long nature trail has 18 sites keyed to an informative booklet; the 2.5-mile overlook trail offers big views of the **Tok River Valley.** From here until **Mentasta Summit,** about 30 miles southwest, watch for wildlife, particularly moose in the ponds, bears along the rivers, and Dall's sheep on the mountainsides.

About 20 miles past the summit awaits the 45-mile **Nabesna Road,** one of only two roads that penetrate deep into America's largest national park and preserve, 13.2 million-acre **Wrangell–St. Elias** *(907-822-5235. Ranger station Mem. Day–Sept.).* This isn't Yosemite Valley. Before proceeding stop at the ranger station just off the highway and find out about recent bear activity, road conditions (usually fine until Mile 29), the mucky trails, and the weather.

Why bother with such a troublesome side trip? Because you may see bears, moose, caribou, and even wolves in the lowland tundra along Nabesna Road. Because you can pull into informal campsites overlooking small lakes sprinkled with waterfowl. Because the muscular peaks of the Wrangell and Mentasta Mountains surround you. Because it's about as wild and unpeopled a place as can be reached by car.

Tok's Miracle Rescue

In 1990 the forest from which Tok is carved nearly reclaimed the townsite. The Great Tok Fire, a 100,000-acre blaze that burned for eight weeks, crackled right to the edge of town. Residents talk about standing in the center of Tok, helplessly watching their huge American flag blowing in the powerful wind that was whipping the fire into town. Suddenly, the flag drooped, then flapped up again but in the opposite direction—the wind had shifted 180 degrees. The fire turned back on itself and burned out.

Into the Interior

Near Nabesna Road the highway joins the **Copper River** and follows it more than 60 miles down to **Gakona Junction;** try not to run off the road as you admire this grand river and the 14,000-foot-plus peaks of the Wrangell Mountains. At the junction, turn north up the Richardson Highway and drive 57 miles to ❺ **Paxson,** enjoying the road's flirtation with the **Gulkana River.** Its west and middle forks have been designated national wild and scenic rivers and are popular with rafters and canoeists.

For a short and rapids-free rafting trip on the Gulkana, hook up with **Paxson Alpine Tours** *(Jct. of Richardson and Denali Hwys. 907-822-5972. Fee).* On summer evenings born-and-bred Alaskans Murray and Kris Howk (or one of their family members) take one or two rafts on a few-hour float down a tranquil, clear-water stretch of the river. It's only about 50 feet wide and maybe 2 to 5 feet deep, creating a feeling of intimacy with the landscape. Spawning sockeye redden the water, dozens of bald eagles hang around for the salmon feast, and passengers sometimes see moose, beavers, muskrats, and the occasional bear.

From Paxson turn west onto the **Denali Highway**★★ *(Glennallen BLM Office 907-822-3217),* a destination in itself as much as a route back to Denali National Park and Preserve. For 135 miles—112 of them unpaved—the highway courses through a dramatic expanse of prime Alaskan wilderness, anchored by the sawtooth, ice-capped wall of the **Alaska Range** to the north. No towns interrupt the landscape's natural beauty. Most of the road lies above tree line, producing panoramic views and a top-of-the-world atmosphere; viewpoints about 6 and 13 miles out of Paxson provoke gasps. At about Mile 21 travelers come down to the **Tangle Lakes**★, an area noted for its hundreds of archaeological sites, some dating back more than 10,000 years.

On a map this area of lakes, ponds, and rivers is largely blue. The lush wetlands and tundra support a wealth of wildlife, including moose, caribou, wolves, bears, otters, and many species of birds. Along with those birds come bird-watchers, who gather at **Tangle Lakes Lodge**★ *(Mile 22. 907-688-9173).* The lodge owners are avid birders and will happily direct people to the nearest Arctic warbler or gyrfalcon. The lodge is ecumenical, however, and also draws hikers, hunters, canoeists, fishermen, bicyclists, and sightseers. Use the spotting scope that sits on the bar to look at grizzlies and the mountains as well as to watch birds. Not unimportant, out here in the middle of nowhere, the lodge also serves excellent meals.

Thirteen miles west of the lodge, the road peaks at

Maclaren Summit, at 4,086 feet the second highest highway pass in Alaska. In June and July, the views and the wildflowers compete for your attention, a contest you can't lose. If you want even more views and flowers,

Tangle Lakes campground

drive another 1.5 miles to the **Maclaren Summit Trailhead** and hike across the tundra.

Starting about 45 miles from Paxson, a series of lakes flank the road for some 10 miles. Many are kettle lakes, left behind when enormous chunks of ice broke off from retreating glaciers and became buried. When the ice melted, the soil slumped down, leaving a kettle-shaped depression that eventually filled with water. Ducks, geese, loons, sandhill cranes, and bald eagles frequent these lakes, as well as scene-stealing trumpeter swans, whose wild blasts put Miles Davis to shame.

From here to ⑥ **Cantwell** there are no particular places to stop—yet there are a thousand places you'll want to pull over and spend some time. Give in to the urge. Beaver lodges dot the ponds and lakes beside the road; sometimes you can watch these industrious rodents meticulously repair their stick-and-mud huts. Short cross-country rambles can yield containers full of blueberries and purple-stained lips. Short side roads lead to isolated campsites above wide rivers or beside a wind-rippled lake. And the views seem infinite, both in number and in the distances they encompass. A scant 6 miles from the end of the road a viewpoint provides a grand view of Mount McKinley, a fitting farewell.

Gulf of Alaska Crescent ★★

● **910 miles, excluding ferry** ● **7 days** ● **Summer**

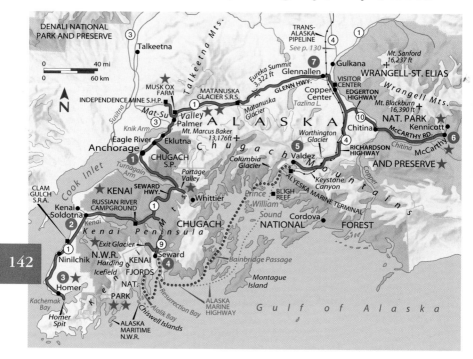

This loop begins in Anchorage, but don't be misled by the familiar urban trappings of Alaska's one semibig city. No town along the drive outside the Anchorage area tops 5,000 in population, and even on the relatively settled Kenai Peninsula you'll see far more forest, wildlife, and lakes than houses and gas stations. The ferry from Seward to Valdez adds to the sense of remoteness as it skirts unspoiled islands and coastline. The wildness reaches its apex at America's largest national park, Wrangell-St. Elias, a 13.2 million-acre sanctuary. From here back to Anchorage the route passes bedraggled taiga forests, huge braided rivers, husky mountains, and Alaska's only significant farmlands. The drive does have civilized moments, however, serving up a number of museums, shops, galleries, and pleasant towns.

Malls, tidy parks, traffic, ❶ **Anchorage** *(Visitor Center 907-276-4118 or 800-478-1255)* offers many of the pros and cons one would find in any American city of 254,000. But it has some differences, starting with the setting: The cold, clean waters of **Cook Inlet** form Anchorage's western border and the snow-draped shoulders of the **Chugach Mountains** bound the city from the east.

To begin understanding the ways in which Anchorage and Alaska differ from the rest of the nation, wander through the **Anchorage Museum of History and Art**★ *(121 W. 7th Ave. 907-343-4326. Closed Mon. mid-Sept.–mid-May; adm. fee).* Most of the ground floor is given to art, historical and modern. Upstairs, you'll find Alaska's past, set up in chronological order from the first crossing of the Bering Land Bridge, perhaps 20,000 years ago, to the present. Many of the artifacts also qualify as art, such as the spooky Haida raven mask with its eerie eyes and the beautiful festival parka made of muskrat, beaver, wolverine, calf, felt, cloth, and glass beads.

143

Anchorage's modern history comes to light at the **Oscar Anderson House** *(420 M St. 907-274-2336. Mid-May–mid-Sept. Tues.-Sat.; adm. fee).* The town began in spring of 1915 as a tent city for railroad workers, and later that year Oscar Anderson built the city's first wood frame house, now restored.

When the kids get squirmy from too much looking and not enough doing, head over to **The Imaginarium Science Discovery Center** *(737 W. 5th Ave. 907-276-3179. Adm. fee).* Children (and adults) can visit a polar bear lair, examine pond scum under microscopes, feel the sticky tentacles of a sea anemone, or blow bubbles to learn how diving beetles carry air underwater.

Anchorage skyline

Imagine landing a small plane on a glacier to rescue mountain climbers or flying through a blizzard to supply a remote outpost. The legendary daring of Alaska's bush pilots is brought to life via videos, photos, artifacts, and some two dozen vintage aircraft at the **Alaska Aviation Heritage Museum** *(4721 Aircraft Dr. 907-248-5325. Mid-May–Sept.; adm. fee),* next to the busy **Lake Hood Seaplane Base.**

Bears still occasionally wander into Anchorage, and spawning salmon still come up **Ship Creek,** in the port area. Stand on the overlook anytime from June through September and you'll probably see chinook, coho, or pinks fighting upstream. The wildness presaged by Ship

Creek begins to emerge soon after you head south on the Seward Highway (Alas. 1). About 10 miles south of town is **Potter Marsh,** a choice patch in the sprawling quilt of the **Anchorage Coastal Wildlife Refuge** *(907-267-2556).* A boardwalk sprinkled with informational signs leads out over the marsh. Salmon school under the boardwalk and birds, including bald eagles, frequent the marsh.

Proceeding along **Turnagain Arm,** travelers soon reach **Beluga Point.** As the name implies, from this turnout one can sometimes spot beluga whales—they're white and look like overgrown bottlenose dolphins, with the same smiles. If your timing is right, you may also see a bore tide, a rushing wall of water as high as 6 feet created when the rising tide starts squeezing into the ever narrowing point of Turnagain Arm. Warning: Don't venture onto the mud-flats of Turnagain Arm at low tide. The water and glacial silt can create something akin to quicksand.

Near the end of Turnagain Arm you can turn off into **Portage Valley**★ *(Chugach National Forest 907-783-3242).* The 5-mile-long Portage Highway leads past ponds favored by moose, a platform providing close views of spawning salmon, two seductive campgrounds, and fine hiking trails. But this valley draws a crowd in summer mainly because the road leads to **Portage Lake,** just below **Portage Glacier,** where aqua-blue icebergs drift in the wind. Want to know why they're blue? Head over to the **Begich, Boggs Visitor Center** *(907-783-2326. Daily Mem. Day–Labor Day, weekends rest of year),* where, among the many displays, you'll learn that glacial ice is so dense that it absorbs the wavelengths of all visible colors except blue, which is reflected back. For a closer look at those icebergs, board the **M.V. *Ptarmigan*** *(Fare)* and slalom through the bergs to the face of the glacier while a Forest Service interpreter elaborates.

Sign near Portage

About 40 miles out of the valley the highway forks, offering two different takes on the **Kenai Peninsula** *(Visitor Center 907-283-3850 or 800-535-3624).* The main route becomes Alas. 9 and continues due south to Seward, while Alas. 1 continues as a 136-mile spur west and south to Homer. To sample one of the many hikes along the spur to Homer, pull into the Russian River Campground of the Chugach National Forest *(907-271-2500)* and head up the **Russian Lakes Trail** *(Parking fee during sockeye season).* The 4-mile round-trip to **Russian River Falls** makes a fine family hike, and the roiling, stair-case rapids of the **Russian River** invites lingering. From

the overlook above the cascades, hikers sometimes can see hundreds of sockeye salmon gathering their strength in the quiet pools *(mid-June–Aug.)*. Every minute or so one will rocket forward, thrashing and leaping in a furious effort to surmount the rapids.

A dramatically different river scene awaits an hour down the highway near ❷ **Soldotna** *(Visitor Center, 44790 Alas. 1. 907-262-1337)*. During much of the summer, hundreds of anglers throng the **Kenai River,** dreaming of besting Soldotna resident Les Andersen, who, in 1985, caught a 97-pound king salmon in the Kenai River, a world-record for sportfishermen. This legendary fish is on display in the Visitor Center.

Soldotna also houses the headquarters of the **Kenai National Wildlife Refuge**★ *(Ski Hill Rd. 2 miles S of town, opposite Sky View High School. 907-262-7021)*. Wildlife displays, films, and a nature trail make the center worth the search. More to the point, visitors can find out how to explore the nearly 2 million-acre refuge, in which they're likely to spot moose, caribou, bald eagles, Dall's sheep, trumpeter swans, and perhaps even a grizzly or black bear. The refuge is noted for its canoe trails.

145

Digging at Clam Gulch State Recreation Area

To the south the highway clings to the shoreline along **Cook Inlet,** affording views of a vast wilderness anchored by 10,000-foot snow-topped volcanoes; one, **Redoubt Volcano,** erupted as recently as the winter of 1989-1990. Residents of **Ninilchik** have enjoyed these views since the early 1800s, and descendants of the founding Russian and native families still live here, most earning a living as commercial fishermen. A walking tour of the village *(map at Ninilchik Village Cache, Mile 135.1 Sterling Hwy.)* climaxes at the lovely Russian Orthodox church atop the hill, complete with a colorful graveyard.

At the highway's end, ❸ **Homer**★ *(Chamber of Commerce 907-235-7740)* has attracted a diverse population of fishermen, artists, shop owners, loggers, and retirees, many drawn by the end-of-the-road atmosphere and the setting on Kachemak Bay. At the **Alaska Maritime National Wildlife Refuge Visitor Center** *(509 Sterling Hwy. 907-235-6961. May–Labor Day)*, polar bear and sea otter pelts, stuffed puffins, a walrus skull complete with 2-foot-long tusks, and other exhibits make this a small museum as well as a Visitor Center. You can watch a variety of videos or join in nearby bird and beach walks with a refuge naturalist.

Downtown, visit the **Pratt Museum**★ *(3779 Bartlett St. 907-235-8635. Closed Jan. and Mon. Oct.-April; adm. fee),* which contains fine natural and human history collections and interesting facts, such as that the gangly giant Pacific octopus has only one little bone and can squeeze through a hole the size of a quarter. Perhaps the museum's finest and most extensive display concerns the *Exxon Valdez* oil spill—take time to listen to the taped comments of the various parties involved, particularly the natives whose subsistence lifestyle was ruined.

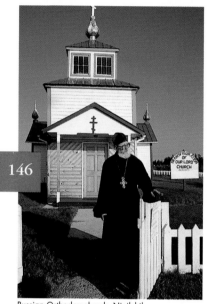

146

Russian Orthodox church, Ninilchik

The **Homer Spit** almost seems like a city unto itself. The last couple of miles of this skinny, 4.5-mile finger of sand sticking out into Kachemak Bay are chockablock with seafood restaurants, shops, boutiques, and in summer hundreds and hundreds of tourists.

From Homer, return to the junction with Alas. 9 and head south toward Seward. These 37 miles of lakes, forests, and mountains almost beseech you to enter on foot. No problem. Several trails of varying difficulty branch out from this section of highway, starting almost 5 miles south of the junction with the **Carter Lake Trail**—look for mountain goats on this steep path *(for information on this and other area trails, contact Seward Ranger District 907-224-3374).* Just before the **Trail Lake Fish Hatchery** is a quarter-mile trail to the platform at the **Moose Creek Fish Viewing Area.**

About 4 miles shy of Seward, turn onto Exit Glacier Road *(mid-May–Oct. Call for conditions),* a 9-mile paved-and-gravel byway that deposits motorists in a corner of **Kenai Fjords National Park**★★ *(Visitor Center, 1212 4th Ave., Seward. 907-224-3175. Closed weekends Labor Day–Mem. Day).* Here on the northeast edge of this 570,000-acre park, you can take several short, easy trails, including one that leads to the base of **Exit Glacier**★. Gaping up at the towering, ragged wave of ice, listening to the low moans as the blue-white behemoth moves ever so slightly, one can almost feel the touch of the ice ages. That era seems even nearer at the end of the strenuous, 3.5-mile trail that winds up to a viewpoint of the **Harding Icefield.** From their perch high in the alpine, hikers can see a chunk of the 700-square-mile expanse of ice. Several flightseeing operations based in Seward can also provide grand views.

When the highway ends at Resurrection Bay, you've arrived in ❹ **Seward** *(Chamber of Commerce 907-224-8051).*

An affable small town, Seward invites lingering at the busy little harbor or strolling along the downtown waterfront. Inextricably linked to the sea, this bayside town teaches its guests about Alaskan waters, especially fish, at the **University of Alaska Fairbanks Seward Marine Education Center** *(125 3rd Ave. 907-224-5261. Mid-May–mid-Sept. Wed.-Sun.)*. Seward's marine education offerings are expected to greatly increase in the spring of 1998, with the opening of the $50-million **Alaska SeaLife Center** *(Railway and 4th Aves. 907-224-3080)*. Though the center will house naturalistic exhibits of marine mammals, fish, seabirds, and other ocean denizens, it will not be an aquarium but a state-of-the-art research and rehabilitation facility with a strong public education mandate.

Brimming with new knowledge about the marine environment, visitors are primed to venture forth along Alaska's spectacular coast aboard one of several tour boats based in Seward. Trips of different lengths are available, but try to

Kenai mountains and glaciers

take a full-day cruise out to the islands and the spectacular fjords that gave the national park its name. Most of the boats fall in the 100-to-200 passenger range and feature snacks and heated viewing decks. One company, **Mariah Tours** *(907-243-1238 or 800-270-1238. Mid-April–Sept.; fare)*, runs two boats that each carry a maximum of only 22 people, offering a more spartan but more personal experience that delves deeper into the area's natural history.

The tours start in **Resurrection Bay,** where sea otters lounge on their backs, bald eagles soar overhead, and bearded mountain goats sometimes appear on the steep slopes of the coastal mountains. As the boat leaves the bay, it's fairly likely you'll see humpback whales; occasionally gray, minke, or killer whales show up.

Usually the boats cruise into **Aialik Bay,** a superb slice of the park's fjord country. The steep, forested slopes on both sides keep the cameras clicking, but the shutters really get popping when the boat reaches one of the active tidewater glaciers being pushed into the sea by the Harding Icefield above. Mariah Tours' boats usually get way back in the bay to **Aialik Glacier,** whose face is a mile wide and very active. At frequent intervals a piece of ice will calve from the glacier, cracking off with gunshot-loud snaps, and bellyflop into the water with a tremendous splash. Sometimes a quarter or even half of the entire face will drop at once, wowing passengers with a sound like a too-near lightning strike and raising a splash that would empty a hundred swimming pools.

Exit Glacier, Kenai Fjords National Park

On the return voyage, tour boats linger at several rugged islands, notably the **Chiswell Islands,** which are part of the **Alaska Maritime National Wildlife Refuge.** From a distance the islands seem engulfed by swarms of gnats, but as the boats draw close those flitting dots turn out to be seabirds—thousands and thousands of them. Among the species that nest on these offshore pinnacles from May through August are murres, auklets, kittiwakes, and the crowd-favorite puffins. Boats approach within a few dozen yards, providing outstanding views of birds preening, squabbling with neighbors, and feeding their young. Supplying the baritone to the birds' soprano are the Steller's sea lions that haul out on the islands.

Now that you have your sea legs, you're ready for the part of the drive that yields great gas mileage: the 12-hour cruise from Seward to Valdez aboard the ferry ***Tustumena*** *(Alaska Marine Highway System 907-465-3941 or 800-642-0066. Fare).* Since it runs only once a week (and the day of the week can change year to year, so check), get reservations months in advance and don't be late. This scenic cruise passes untouched islands and steep, heavily forested coastline. Passengers spot sea otters, seabirds, and sometimes killer whales. The eastbound ferry usually passes through beautiful **Bainbridge Passage** and near the immense **Columbia Glacier.**

Seward Harbor

Good Friday has been a bad day in the history of **⑤ Valdez** *(Convention & Visitors Bureau, 200 Chenega St. 907-835-2984 or 800-770-5954).* As the ferry enters Valdez Arm it passes Bligh Reef, where the *Exxon Valdez* ran aground on Good Friday in 1989 and disgorged nearly 11 million gallons of oil. When the ferry docks in Valdez, it's tying up at a new terminal in a new town; on Good Friday in 1964 the century's second strongest earthquake destroyed the old docks. Visitors can learn about the earthquake by watching a riveting film *(mid-May–mid-Sept.)* shown by the Visitors Bureau (see sidebar p. 151).

The *Exxon Valdez* disaster is examined at the **Valdez Museum**★ *(217 Egan Dr. 907-835-2764. Closed Sun.-Mon. mid-Oct.–mid-April; adm. fee).* The museum covers far more than the oil spill. Spend an hour or two among exhibits on bush pilots, marine life, Eskimos, glaciers (you can touch a piece of the Columbia Glacier that sits in a cooler), the Klondike gold rush, and the Trans-Alaska Pipeline.

The pipeline that conveys Alaskan crude 800 miles from Alaska's North Slope ends at the **Alyeska Marine Terminal,** across the bay from Valdez. Tours start at the **Alyeska Pipeline Visitor Center** *(Valdez Airport. 907-835-2686. Fee for tours),* where exhibits bristle with gee-whiz facts: The pipeline makes some 800 river and stream crossings and weighs 550,000 tons, and so on. From the center a bus takes you to the terminal where gargantuan loading arms dump up to 100,000 barrels of oil an hour into tankers.

A different sort of marine terminal can be found at the Chugach National Forest's **Crooked Creek Information Site** *(Richardson Hwy. 1 mile E of downtown Valdez. 907-835-4680. Mem. Day–Labor Day).* Here chum and pink salmon terminate their ocean journey, spawning in the gravel beds beside the little Visitor Center. On a given summer day *(mid-July–Sept.)* hundreds of salmon will be fighting for territory, fanning the gravel to create nests, laying eggs, and dying. From the platform visitors get unexcelled views. It's just a few feet from the hubbub and the water in the creek is clear and shallow—so shallow that the bulging backs of the "humpies" (male pink salmon develop humps during spawning) stick up above the surface.

Continue the loop by continuing east on the Richardson Highway. If you don't actually pull over, at least slow down in **Keystone Canyon** and admire the several tall waterfalls. And at least pull over if you don't actually get out of the car some 7 miles later at **Blueberry Lake State Recreation Site** *(907-745-3975),* or a few miles farther at **Thompson Pass,** to enjoy the sweeping vistas. You're in alpine tundra here, although the pass is only 2,772 feet high. A couple of miles past the pass definitely stop and get out of your car to see **Worthington Glacier.** Short

View from *Tustumena* between Seward and Valdez

trails lead to within a few feet of the glacier and a covered viewing area features interpretive displays.

Not far from here the highway swings north through steep mountains and forests. About 55 miles past the glacier take the Edgerton Highway, a 33-mile spur road that follows the mighty **Copper River** southeast to Chitina,

and the **McCarthy Road.** There's a mystique about this road, partly because it winds through prime Alaskan wilderness, but mostly because it is flamboyantly lousy for a road that still can be managed by regular passenger cars.

For starters, the road is dirt, much of it washboarded. It's also narrow. When first-time visitors come upon vehicles plunged into roadside shrubbery, they jump out to see if anyone has been injured in the crash. But there hasn't been an accident—locals park that way to get their cars off the skinny road. The road also crosses several small streams without benefit of culverts. Worst of all, the road eats tires. In addition to its crop of pointy rocks, the road runs on top of an old railroad bed that occasionally produces spikes and other sharp metal debris.

Figuring that discretion is the better part of valor, some visitors opt for the shuttle vans that operate out of Chitina and Glennallen. If you intend to brave the highway on your own, stop at the **Chitina Ranger Station** *(907-823-2205. Mem. Day–Labor Day)* and inquire about current road conditions. Allow about three hours one-way and consider bringing two spare tires. Rental car drivers take note of the big sign at the start of the McCarthy Road that instructs you to call your insurance agent before proceeding— guess who's responsible for any damage incurred.

So what's the big attraction that motivates motorists to challenge this execrable road? For one, the town of McCarthy. For another, the historic mining town of Kennicott, now a virtual ghost town. Finally, the McCarthy/Kennicott area lies within **Wrangell-St. Elias National Park and Preserve**★ *(907-822-5235)*; it's the only settled area to speak of within the park (see Into the Interior drive, p. 130).

The isolation of ❻ **McCarthy**★ is underscored by the fact that motorists must leave their cars on the west side of the Kennicott River and cross over to this town of 30 by pulling themselves hand-over-hand above the river in a small cable tram. (A footbridge may be built soon.)

On a given summer day perhaps a hundred people will be in McCarthy, signing up for flightseeing trips, glacier treks, river rafting, or just hanging out. This tourist activity has brought additions to the town, such as a couple of small historic hotels, a good restaurant, and even a pizza place, but these few amenities fit in pretty well and have not drastically altered its back-of-beyond essence. Stop by the little historical museum, which brims with intriguing details, such as the program for the town's 1929 Fourth of July events, noting what

Bad Friday in Valdez

The Good Friday 1964 earthquake struck Valdez hard, as is evident in the film shown by the Visitors Bureau. Especially chilling is the 8mm footage shot by a deck hand aboard the steamer *Chena*, which was tied to the Valdez dock when the quake wrenched the earth, its epicenter just 40 miles away. The grainy film shows deck hands tossing candy and fruit to kids on the dock when suddenly the piers and the beach slide violently into the ocean. The *Chena* bounced off the bottom of the bay and swept into town and back on a tsunami, yet somehow it stayed afloat and only two crew members were killed. All 30 persons on the docks died. The savaged town was abandoned and a site on safer ground 4 miles away was chosen for the new Valdez.

151

Bear Savvy

Bear attacks are rare, but they do happen, even within 10 miles of Anchorage. Be prepared: First, don't attract bears to your picnic or campsite. Leave smelly and greasy foods at home, cook and store food at least 100 yards downwind from camp, and don't wear perfumes or scented deodorants—smell human, not delicious. Second, make noise, as most bear attacks occur when bears are surprised: Have loud arguments, wear bells, or sing. Third, if you encounter a bear, don't run. Speak in a low, calm voice and back away. If it charges …well, for the whole story on bear safety, contact the Alaska Public Lands Information Center in Anchorage (907-271-2737).

must have been a riveting nail-driving contest for "Ladies" and a 50-yard dash for "Fat Men."

About 4 miles up a dirt road from McCarthy lies the old copper-mining town of **Kennicott★**, where the Kennecott Mines Company operated from 1906 to 1938. (The different spellings are because the company misspelled the name of the Alaska explorer after whom the valley's glacier was named.) Dozens of structures remain reasonably intact, offering visitors the chance to nose around in Alaska's mining past. Energetic visitors can hike for miles up along the Kennicott and Root Glaciers. Those who wish to lounge around and inhale the raw beauty of the park can relax on the 180-foot-long front porch of the **Kennicott Glacier Lodge** *(907-258-2350 or 800-582-5128. Mid-May–mid-Sept.).* A van *(fare)* shuttles people between McCarthy and Kennicott.

Back on the Richardson Highway, continue north about 18 miles and take the **Old Richardson Highway** through the historic town of **Copper Center.** Stop at the **George I. Ashby Memorial Museum** *(Mile 101 Richardson Hwy. Loop Rd. 907-822-3245. June-Aug. Mon.-Sat.),* its two log cabins awash in pioneer and native artifacts. Four miles later lies **Wrangell-St. Elias National Park and Preserve Headquarters and Visitor Center** *(Mile 105 Richardson Highway Loop Rd. 907-822-5235. Closed weekends Labor Day–Mem. Day),* where you can gather information.

A mile farther the road rejoins the main Richardson Highway. Go about 8 miles north to a viewpoint of the **Wrangell Mountains,** including a couple of 16,000-foot peaks. Just over 2 miles along lies ⑦ **Glennallen** *(Greater Copper River Valley Visitor Information Center 907-822-5555),* the service hub for the sprawling **Copper River Basin.**

Turn west on the Glenn Highway, and proceed through miles and miles of taiga, the Russian word for "land of little sticks." The scrawny conifers that manage to survive in this cold, wet, northernmost forest zone tend to lean at crazy angles, hence the label many Alaskans use: "drunken forest." In about an hour's drive, the highway climbs out of the taiga and into the mountains. Numerous hiking trails branch off the highway between here and the Matanuska-Susitna Valley. Keep your binoculars handy, because you'll soon start getting views of the **Matanuska Glacier.** Of course, one hardly needs help to

Hand-powered cable tram crossing the Kennicott River

Kennecott Mine site, Wrangell-St. Elias National Park and Preserve

see this ice age relic; it's 27 miles long and 4 miles across at the terminus. At the **Matanuska Glacier State Recreation Site** you can gaze down upon the glacier from cliff-top platforms. By looking back and forth from the diagrams on the interpretive signs to the glacier itself, observers will finally understand exactly what cirques and moraines are.

Fifty miles through broad-shouldered mountains along the wide braids of the **Matanuska River** bring motorists to Alaska's breadbasket, the **Matanuska-Susitna** or **Mat-Su Valley**★★ *(Convention & Visitors Bureau 907-746-5000)*. For a bucolic scene with a twist, turn off on Archie Road and tour the **Musk Ox Farm**★ *(Mile 50.1 Glenn Hwy., Palmer. 907-745-4151. Mid-May–Sept.; adm. fee)*. Musk oxen look odd, like a cross between a cape buffalo and a Lhasa apso. Visitors on the guided tour will see many exhibits and dozens of musk oxen in the flesh—tons of flesh, as these brutes average about 600 pounds each. Sometimes they play "musk ox football," which involves shoving around a 500-pound ball (see sidebar p. 155).

Gold. That magic metal lured miners into the Talkeetna Mountains just north of the Mat-Su Valley in the early 1900s. An echo of that boom entices today's travelers off the highway half a mile past Musk Ox Farm and up into those mountains to see the long-abandoned but largely intact mining complex at **Independence Mine State Historical Park** *(Mile 17.3 on the Hatcher Pass Rd./Palmer-Fishhook Rd. 907-745-2827. Depending on weather, guided* *tours daily June–Labor Day; adm. fee).* Start with the exhibits in the Visitor Center (the former manager's house). Anyone romanticizing the life of a miner should consider the photos from deep in the mines and the sheet that shows wages—a mucker raked in a whopping 93 cents an hour. From the Visitor Center, you can walk to the commissary, bunkhouses, the mess hall, the assay office (which is also a museum), and many other buildings. Longer trails lead to the mine area and to a gem of an alpine lake.

For a taste of the Mat-Su Valley, return to the Glenn Highway and drive 7 miles to the valley's agricultural heart, **Palmer** *(Chamber of Commerce and Visitor Center, S. Valley Way and Fireweed St. 907-745-2880. Visitor Center May–mid-Sept.).* Although the growing season is only 80 to 110 days, the midnight sun helps create record-setting produce. Wander the **Matanuska Valley Agricultural Showcase** beside the Visitor Center and take in the wealth of fruits, herbs, flowers, and vegetables, including those famed hundred-pound cabbages. If your mouth begins to water, you can buy fresh Mat-Su produce across the street at the **Palmer Farmers' Market.** The Palmer area harbors many u-pick farms and produce stands, as well.

Glenn Highway, near Glennallen

In 1935 the agricultural potential of the valley motivated FDR's New Deal planners to initiate the Matanuska Valley Colony Project. To provide a fresh start for farmers hit hard by the Depression and to populate Alaska, the government recruited some 200 midwestern families and brought them to the Mat-Su Valley. What is now Palmer was built by the colonists and government workers as their central town. The **Colony Museum** in the Visitor Center's basement tells of their struggle and eventual triumph. Maps show how to reach some of the remaining colony buildings and farms, including the handsome log **Church of a Thousand Trees** and the farms in the pretty **Bodenburg Butte** area.

A far older town lies some 17 miles down the Glenn Highway from Palmer. **Eklutna Historical Park** *(907-696-2828. Mid-May–mid-Sept.; adm. fee)* preserves an Athapaskan settlement heavily influenced by Russian culture dating back to the 1600s. Guided tours through the museum and the grounds take in displays of native art (note the exquisite bead work), the 1830s-vintage **St. Nicholas Russian Orthodox Church,** and the native cemetery, whose graves are decorated by brightly colored spirit houses.

Just 13 miles from Anchorage, travelers can turn off into downtown **Eagle River** and follow Eagle River Road another 12 miles to some prime Alaskan wilderness in **Chugach State Park.** The park road ends at the **Eagle River Nature Center** *(907-694-2108).* In this former roadhouse, visitors can peruse exhibits, get information on the half-million-acre park, and gaze through a spotting scope at Dall's sheep and other wildlife. Several hiking trails fan out from the center, permitting travelers one last dance with wild Alaska before they return to Anchorage.

155

Qiviut

Musk oxen are the quintessential Arctic animal, built to withstand horrendous cold. They have hair everywhere, from the edges of their lips to their hooves. And not just any hair, but qiviut, considered the warmest in the world, eight times warmer than sheep's wool by weight. There are a handful of places in Alaska where visitors can buy clothing made from qiviut, including the Musk Ox Farm in Palmer. Farm employees comb the qiviut from the musk oxen and ship it to remote Eskimo villages, where it is knit by hand into luxuriously warm, sumptuously soft, and exceedingly expensive garments.

U.S. Forest Service Information center for Washington and Oregon *503-872-2750*. Information center for Alaska *907-586-8751*. Campground reservations for all 50 states *800-280-2267*.

OREGON
Oregon Tourism *800-547-7842*. General state tourism information.
Dept. of Fish & Wildlife *503-872-5268*. Hunting and fishing information and licensing.
Oregon Outdoor Association *800-747-9552*. Information on Oregon outfitters.
State Parks Information *800-551-6949*. General information on Oregon's state parks.
Crater Lake National Park *541-594-2211*.

WASHINGTON
Washington State Tourism *360-586-2088* or *800-638-8474*.
Dept. of Fish & Wildlife General questions *360-902-2200*. Licensing for hunting and fishing *360-902-2464*.
State Parks Information *800-233-0321*. General information on Washington's state parks.
Washington State Ferries *206-464-6400* or *800-843-3779* (Wash. only). Schedules, fees, and destinations.
Bed & Breakfast Reservation Service *206-439-7677*.
Mount Rainier National Park *360-569-2211*.
North Cascades National Park *360-856-5700*.
Olympic National Park *360-452-0330*.

ALASKA
Alaska Division of Tourism *907-465-2010*. Vacation planner including accommodation, recreation, and bush plane information.
Alaska Ferry Information *800-642-0066* (U.S.) and *800-665-6414* (Canada). Alaska Marine Highway information.
Dept. of Fish & Game All hunting inquiries including licenses *907-465-4190*. All fishing inquiries including licenses *907-465-4180*.
Road Information *907-273-6037*. Recorded up-to-date road conditions.
Bed & Breakfast Reservations and Packaged Tours *907-337-3414*.
Denali National Park and Preserve *907-683-2294*.
Kenai Fjords National Park *907-224-3175*.
Wrangell–St. Elias National Park and Preserve *907-822-5235*.

HOTEL & MOTEL CHAINS
(Accommodations in all three states unless otherwise noted)

Best Western International *800-528-1234*
Choice Hotels *800-4-CHOICE*
Clarion Hotels *800-CLARION* (except Alas.)
Comfort Inns *800-228-5150*
Courtyard by Marriott *800-321-2211* (except Alas.)
Days Inn *800-325-2525*
Doubletree Hotels and Guest Suites *800-222-TREE* (except Alas.)
Econo Lodge *800-446-6900* (except Alas.)
Embassy Suites *800-EMBASSY* (except Alas.)
Fairfield Inn by Marriott *800-228-2800* (except Alas.)
Hampton Inn *800-HAMPTON* (except Alas.)
Hilton Hotels *800-HILTONS*
Holiday Inns *800-HOLIDAY*
Howard Johnson *800-654-2000* (except Alas.)
Hyatt Hotels and Resorts *800-233-1234* (Wash. only)
Marriott Hotels Resorts Suites *800-228-9290*
Motel 6 *800-466-8356* (except Alas.)
Quality Inns-Hotels-Suites *800-228-5151*
Radisson Hotels International *800-333-3333* (Washington only)
Ramada Inns *800-2-RAMADA*
Red Lion Hotels, Inc. *800-547-8010* (except Alas.)
Sheraton Hotels & Inns *800-325-3535*
Super 8 Motels *800-843-1991*
Vagabond Inns *800-522-1555* (except Alas.)
Westin Hotels and Resorts *800-228-3000*

ILLUSTRATIONS CREDITS

Photographs in this book are by Phil Schofield, except for the following: 8 Chris Johns, National Geographic Photographer; 81 Bruce Heinemann/The Stock Market; 109 Richard A. Cooke III; 123 (upper) John Marshall; 131 (lower) Patrick Powell; 132-133 Stefan Schott/Ken Graham Agency; 134 (lower), 135, 143 Ken Graham/Ken Graham Agency.

NOTES ON AUTHOR AND PHOTOGRAPHER

After many visits to the Pacific Northwest, Bob Devine finally moved there in 1990, settling in Oregon. He has contributed to several National Geographic books and written numerous articles for National Geographic Traveler. Currently he is writing a book on non-native species for the Society.

Northwest photographer Phil Schofield lives with his wife, Susan, and two childen, Eiron and Russ, overlooking the San Juan Islands. His 20 years of specializing in editorial and travel photography for a wide variety of U.S. and foreign publications has allowed him to explore and photograph some of the most beautiful and remote places on earth. Phil's work often appears in National Geographic publications.

Index

157

Index

160

Composition for this book by the National Geographic Society Book Division. Printed and bound by R.R. Donnelly & Sons, Willard, Ohio. Color separations by Digital Color Image, Pensauken, New Jersey. Paper by Consolidated/Alling & Cory, Willow Grove, Pennsylvania. Cover printed by Miken Companies, Inc. Cheektowaga, New York.

Library of Congress Cataloging-in-Publication Data

Devine, Bob, 1951-
Pacific Northwest, Oregon, Washington, and Alaska / by Bob Devine; photographs by Phil Schofield.
p.   cm. — (National Geographic's driving guides to America)
Includes index.
ISBN 0-7922-3429-4
1. Northwest, Pacific—Tours. 2. Alaska—Tours. 3. Automobile travel—Northwest, Pacific—Guidebooks. 4. Automobile travel—Alaska—Guidebooks.   I. Schofield, Phil.   II. Title.   III. Series.
F852.3.D48 1997
917.9504'43—dc21   97-5864
                                                           CIP

Visit the Society's Web site at www.nationalgeographic.com